Florida

OFF THE BEATEN PATH™

"A pleasantly low-key guide to more than 1,000 lesser-known sites worth a detour . . ."
   —Robert Jenkins, *St. Petersburg Times*

"Authors Bill and Diana Gleasner have been enjoying Florida for more than thirty years and their intimate knowledge reflects virtually every corner of this popular winter state."
   —Gordon Charles, syndicated travel writer

"Offers descriptions of unique attractions often missed by travelers to Florida."
   —*Michigan Living*

"This book is . . . a good item to keep in the glove compartment so that it will be available during those all-important times when you're seeking an unplanned, spontaneous adventure. . . ."
   —*Sunday Advocate, Vacation & Travel Special Edition,*
      Baton Rouge

Florida

OFF THE
BEATEN
PATH™

FOURTH EDITION

DIANA AND
BILL GLEASNER

A Voyager Book

Old Saybrook, Connecticut

Cover map © DeLorme Mapping
Text illustrations by Carol Drong

Library of Congress Cataloging-in-Publication Data
Gleasner, Diana C.
    Florida : off the beaten path / Diana and Bill Gleasner. — 4th ed.
       p.   cm. — (Off the beaten path series)
    "A Voyager book."
    Includes index.
    ISBN 1-56440-961-9
    1. Florida—Guidebooks. I. Gleasner, Bill. II. Title. III. Series.
F309.3.G55   1996
917.5904'63—dc20
                                                 96-16224
                                                   CIP

Manufactured in the United States of America
Fourth Edition/Second Printing

To Ed and Susan Cottle—
Intrepid Florida Explorers

FLORIDA

NORTHWEST

NORTHEAST

CENTRAL

SOUTHEAST

SOUTHWEST

THE KEYS

CONTENTS

ACKNOWLEDGMENTS

Many thanks to the Florida Division of Tourism.

To our able assistants, Audrey Templeton and Patsy Kiszely, a round of grateful applause.

Also, thanks to Andy Newman.

INTRODUCTION

Warning! Straying from the beaten interstate can be addictive. But is it ever fun!

By poking and prowling around this incredible state, we discovered a high rise for bats, the world's smallest police station, a McDonald's complete with salt licks and hitching posts, a museum dedicated to the inventor of air-conditioning, and an Arctic blizzard (Eglin Air Force Base Climatic Laboratory). Florida seems to have cornered the "world's largest" market. We saw the largest concentration of saw grass, the largest bald cypress tree, and the largest collections of Frank Lloyd Wright buildings, Art Deco buildings, Salvador Dali artworks, and Tiffany glass in the world. We even strolled the world's longest continuous sidewalk.

We traveled by inner tube, pontoon boat, car, motor home, houseboat, sailboat, seaplane, canoe, motorized gondola, and airboat. Our meanderings took us through Little Havana, the Greek community of Tarpon Springs, and a Miccosukee Indian Village.

We heard a dolphin take a deep breath in the Everglades, toured a thoroughbred farm, and chatted with a cow hunter rounding up one of the few remaining herds of scrub cattle in existence. We saw a tapir, manatees, wood storks, a herd of buffalo, and alligators romping in the surf!

We slept in a lighthouse, cheered ourselves hoarse at a rodeo, hunted for fossil shark teeth, lunched in an indoor swimming pool (luckily for us, it was dry), nibbled on alligator tail (lucky for us, it was not connected to anyone), and pitched a tent on more than a few of the Ten Thousand Islands.

In short, we have enjoyed an abundance of serendipitous experiences. But there are many more discoveries waiting to be made in Florida. Write us (c/o The Globe Pequot Press, P.O. Box 833, Old Saybrook, CT 06475) and tell us your special finds.

Travel safely and have a terrific time!

Here are a few addresses that will come in handy. We especially recommend sending for the state parks brochure so you can take advantage of one of the most marvelous state park systems in the country.

INTRODUCTION

General Information
Florida Chamber of Commerce
P.O. Box 11309
Tallahassee, FL 32302
(904) 425-1200

Florida Division of Tourism
Visitor Inquiry
107 W. Gaines Street
Tallahassee, FL 32399
(904) 487-1462

Historical Resources
R. A. Gray Building
500 S. Bronough Street
Tallahassee, FL 32399
(904) 487-2333

State Parks
Florida Department of Natural Resources
Division of Recreation and Parks
Bureau of Education and Information
3900 Commonwealth Boulevard
Tallahassee, FL 32303
(904) 488-7326

The prices and rates listed in this guidebook were confirmed at press time. We recommend, however, that you call establishments before traveling to obtain current information.

NORTHEAST FLORIDA

1–7 Amelia Island

Jacksonville

8–15
Jacksonville
Area

29

28

Gainesville Area
Gainesville

25–27
24

23

St. Augustine

St. Augustine
Area
16–21

22

1. Centre Street Fernandina
2. Palace Saloon
3. Bailey House
4. Fort Clinch State Park
5. Seahorse Stable
6. Lighthouse lodging
7. Amelia Island Plantation
8. Little Talbot Island State Park
9. Kingsley Plantation
10. U.S. Naval Station
11. Fort Caroline National Memorial
12. Riverwalk
13. Museum of Science and History
14. Alexander Brest Planetarium
15. Cummer Museum of Art and Gardens
16. Castillo de San Marcos

17. St. George Street
18. Spanish Quarter
19. Lightner Museum
20. Cafe Alcazar
21. The Conch House Restaurant
22. Bulow Plantation Ruins Historic Site
23. Palatka Ravine State Ornamental Garden
24. Marjorie Kinnan Rawlings State Historic Site
25. Payne's Prairie State Preserve
26. Florida Museum of Natural History
27. Devil's Millhopper State Geological Site
28. O'Leno State Park
29. Ichetucknee Springs State Park

Northeast Florida

Amelia Island

Amelia Island, with its 13 miles of uncrowded sandy beaches, has already been discovered. In fact, it is the only United States location to have been under eight different flags: French, Spanish, British, American Patriots (1812), Green Cross of Florida (1817), Mexican, Confederate, and United States.

The Timucuan Indians' simple life was disrupted first by the French in the sixteenth century and then by the Spanish. The Union Jack was raised in 1763, but the Tories who converged on the island during the Revolutionary War left when Florida was ceded to Spain. A military adventurer, General Sir Gregor MacGregor, captured the island and claimed it as his for a brief time but was ousted by a pirate who took over ostensibly for Mexico. After the United States government took formal possession, the claim was disputed by the Confederacy, which raised its flag here during the Civil War.

Federal occupation during the Civil War triggered a tourist boom. This, with an impressive flow of money created by the shipping business, made Fernandina Beach a prosperous community. Before long, handsome Victorian homes lined the residential streets. These architectural gems, dating from 1857 and ranging in style from old steamboat Gothic to Queen Anne, earned the 30-block Old Town district, also known as ✦ **Centre Street Fernandina,** a listing on the National Register of Historic Places. Be sure to stop at the chamber of commerce near the city docks for walking or driving tour directions to this gingerbread seaport.

It was from these docks that the country's first offshore shrimp trawlers sailed early in this century. For a look at the multicolored shrimp nets being made, go through the back door of **Standard Marine Supply Corporation** on Alachua Street. This father-and-son operation does not offer a formal tour, but keep in mind that Fernandina Beach is the only town in the country that has a shrimp net manufacturer on site to accommodate the fleet. Be sure to be at the docks at sunset to watch the shrimping fleet return with the day's catch.

Stroll past the old ❖ **Palace Saloon,** or better yet, stop in to inspect its splendid carved mahogany bar, which a reliable source has called "the best bar east of Boise." Be sure to sample a mini-platter of fresh boiled shrimp while enjoying local color in the

Palace Saloon

3

oldest saloon in Florida. The Palace Saloon is on the corner of Second and Centre; (904) 261–6320.

Historic Centre Street bristles with fascinating shops and boutiques. **The Ships Lantern** (210 Centre Street) offers a fine selection of paintings, prints, woodcarvings, scrimshaw, and jewelry made from shark teeth found in the area.

If you would like to stock up on gourmet jelly and marinated asparagus, the **Cross-Eyed Bear** (201 Centre Street) is the place to satisfy your gourmet cravings.

Even if you don't stay in the ◆ **Bailey House,** be sure to take a good look at this 1895 Victorian bed-and-breakfast inn in the heart of the historic district. Its turrets, gables, bays, fish-scale decoration, and stained glass windows make it a showcase. No wonder it cost $10,000—an outrageous amount in 1895! The rooms are filled with carved furniture, brass beds, pump organs, fringed lamps, and footed bathtubs, and guests are served a continental breakfast in the elegant dining room. No children, pets, or smoking in the building. Located at 28 Seventh Street, the Bailey House address is P.O. Box 805, Fernandina Beach, FL 32034; (904) 261–5390 or (800) 251–5390.

◆ **Fort Clinch State Park** on Atlantic Avenue in Fernandina Beach welcomes visitors to the most northeasterly point in Florida. Its European-style brick masonry is unique in this country, and you'll get a splendid view of the Atlantic Ocean and Georgia's Cumberland Island from the fort's ramparts. On the first full weekend of every month, rangers reenact the 1864 occupation in full period costume. The park's recreation facilities include saltwater fishing (1,500-foot lighted pier), swimming, camping, picnicking, and hiking. The park, which is on Atlantic Avenue in Fernandina Beach (off SR A1A), opens at 8:00 A.M. and closes at sunset year-round. Fort Clinch State Park, 2601 Atlantic Avenue, Fernandina Beach, FL 32034; (904) 277–7274.

Amelia Island is one of the last spots on the Atlantic seaboard where you can ride horseback on the beach. Rides go out daily, weather permitting, and last approximately one and a quarter hours. Inexperienced riders should not hesitate; ◆ **Seahorse Stable** has a gentle horse for you. The stable is located on First Coast Highway at the south end of the island. For reservations call (904) 261–4878.

If you've always wanted to stay in a ◆ **lighthouse** right on the

4

beach, this is your chance. Four floors include two bedrooms (sleeps up to four), two baths, a kitchen and dining area, and an observation deck for expansive viewing of the great Atlantic Ocean. Wallpapered in nautical charts, this is the place for faraway dreams. Breakfast and the morning paper are delivered to your door. The lighthouse is on the ocean side of SR A1A on the northern end of Amelia Island. Write to Amelia Island Lodging Systems, 584 South Fletcher, Amelia Island, FL 32034; (904) 261–4148.

Bailey House

5

◆ **Amelia Island Plantation** is a low-key, four-star resort offering a wide range of accommodations and amenities ranging from a beautiful beach and complete health club to a well-supervised children's program. Tennis enthusiasts have the run of twenty-five courts at **Plantation Racket Club,** and golfers play on forty-five challenging holes, which architect Pete Dye claims are the only true links on the East Coast. The fishing is fine whether it's deep-sea tarpon and kingfish charter, freshwater lagoon angling, or crabbing.

Nature lovers should follow the **Plantation's Sunken Forest Trail.** The dense semitropical growth includes palms, magnolias, and live oaks festooned with Spanish moss. About a quarter of this resort community has been set aside as a nature preserve enjoyed by raccoons, opossums, armadillos, and alligators.

Amelia Island Plantation's Pool Villas provide the last word on romantic getaways. Imagine rolling out of bed and into your own private indoor swimming pool in a villa hidden deep in a moss-draped forest. Add a nearby beach and candlelight dinners overlooking the ocean, and you have the ingredients of a perfect lovers' retreat. The Plantation is on the southern end of Amelia Island off U.S. A1A, 29 miles northeast of Jacksonville International Airport. Amelia Island Plantation, Amelia Island, FL 32034-1330; (800) 874–6878.

JACKSONVILLE AREA

◆ **Little Talbot Island State Park** embraces a quiet curving beach hidden beyond the dunes and framed by graceful sea oats. This is a delightful spot to camp, swim, and picnic on an unspoiled beach. Open 8:00 A.M. to sunset year-round. Little Talbot Island is 17 miles northeast of Jacksonville, off SR A1A; (904) 251–2320.

The house at ◆ **Kingsley Plantation,** believed to be the oldest plantation house in Florida, has been restored in pre–Civil War style. Long rows of crumbling quarters are a mute reminder of the days of slavery. Open 9:00 A.M.–5:00 P.M. daily. This national park is on Fort George Island, off SR A1A; (904) 251–3537.

The **Marine Science Education Center** welcomes visitors to a marine museum, wet lab (with more than a dozen different aquaria), and a collection of marine specimens including everything from giant clam shells to huge whale vertebrae. The center, in the historic village of Mayport, is 1 block south of the ferry slip on SR A1A (1347 Palmer Street). The reason the center looks like a school is because it is one. Although this resource is primarily for students, visitors are welcome 8:00 A.M.–2:30 P.M. Monday through Friday except school holidays; (904) 247–5973.

◈ **U.S. Naval Station** (on Mayport Road) at Mayport is home port for giant aircraft carriers as well as many smaller ships. Tours are given Tuesday through Friday. Ask at the gate for ship location or phone the Public Affairs Officer at (904) 270–5226. For an information-packed pre-recorded message, call (904) 270–NAVY.

◈ **Fort Caroline National Memorial** commemorates the only French attempt to establish a colony in Florida (1564). The 138-acre park features exhibits, guided tours, and an interpretive model of the original fort. The story told is a tragic one, ending in the massacre of most of the French settlers by the Spanish from St. Augustine. Located about 5 miles from the mouth of the St. Johns River. Open daily 9:00 A.M.–5:00 P.M. Fort Caroline National Memorial, 12713 Fort Caroline Road, Jacksonville, FL 32225; (904) 641–7155. Free.

Jacksonville is Florida's largest and most populous city as well as its leading financial, industrial, transportation, and commercial center. Situated on a bend in the St. Johns River, this bustling and prosperous port is a skyscrapered showcase of sophisticated urban amenities. The St. Johns, the only major river in the United States to flow from south to north, has been the focus of the city's development since Jacksonville was founded in 1822. An ambitious riverfront beautification program has spiffed up the south bank with its attractive ◈ **Riverwalk.** Be sure to stroll the boardwalk and enjoy a fine view of this bustling city.

Adjacent to the Riverwalk are several fine restaurants, an excellent museum, and one of the world's tallest fountains, which erupts after dark into a spirited rainbow of beautiful colors. The ◈ **Museum of Science and History** is a treasure house of exploration for the whole family. Attractions include a 28-foot dinosaur skeleton, an exhibit of Florida Indian culture, and the ◈ **Alexander Brest Planetarium** with its daily multimedia productions. The museum is at 1025 Museum Circle in Jack-

7

sonville. Open Monday through Friday 10:00 A.M.–5:00 P.M., Saturday 10:00 A.M.–6:00 P.M., and Sunday 1:00–6:00 P.M.; (904) 396–7061.

How grand to be able to promenade the Riverwalk, explore the museum, and then satisfy your appetite in style. **Crawdaddy's** looks like a disaster from the outside, but that's part of its charm. The front yard of this ramshackle fish-camp shanty features rusting skeletons of old cars, a rooster, and chickens. Beneath the corrugated tin roof you'll find a fine restaurant. Try an appetizer of Florida alligator chased by beer cheese soup, Cajun chicken, and upside-down apple walnut pie. Crawdaddy's is at 1643 Prudential Drive, Jacksonville. Most dinner entrees range from moderate to expensive; (904) 396–3546.

The ❖ **Cummer Museum of Art and Gardens** features sculpture in a lovely formal garden setting, a permanent collection of Old Masters, and a 720-piece collection of early Meissen Porcelain at 829 Riverside Avenue, Jacksonville. Open Tuesday through Friday 10:00 A.M.–4:00 P.M., Saturday noon–5:00 P.M., Sunday 2:00–5:00 P.M., and Tuesday evening 4:00–9:30 P.M.; (904) 356–6857. Free.

The brew-master's art is on display at the **Anheuser-Busch Brewery.** After your tour enjoy a free taste of the product or soft drinks in the hospitality room. Take I–95 north to the Busch Drive exit. The brewery is at 111 Busch Drive, Jacksonville. Self-guiding and conducted tours are available 9:00 A.M.–4:00 P.M. Monday through Saturday; (904) 751–8118. Free.

Ever dream of chocolate? **Peterbrooke Chocolatier** has the answer to your dreams. The store overflows with chocolate tennis rackets, golf balls, and teddy bears. The candy is made from a secret recipe (known only to three people), and you may view the hand dipping on the premises.

The specialty here is fresh creme truffles, but you may also indulge yourself in chocolate-smothered oreos, chocolate-covered popcorn, fresh strawberries dipped in chocolate, or ice cream appropriately named Total Decadence (loaded with milk chocolate, semisweet chocolate, and macadamia nuts).

The chocolatier ships products all over the world but maintains a keen interest in the local community. Peterbrooke was the inspiration for much of the impressive restoration of the San Marco area, and you will want to visit other shops and restaurants in the area. Peterbrooke is at 2024 San Marco Boulevard, Jacksonville, FL 32207; (904) 398–2488.

St. Augustine Area

St. Augustine, 40 miles south of Jacksonville, is an important repository of history, not only for the community and the state but for the entire nation. In a cheerful if sometimes unsettling mix, the city's carefully preserved past rubs shoulders with the most blatant commercialism, but it is impossible not to be impressed by the city's antiquity. A history that spans four centuries covers a lot of territory.

Ponce de Leon, landing in this general vicinity, claimed the region for Spain, but it was Pedro Menendez de Aviles, sent by the King of Spain to get rid of the French, who established the first settlement. Continuously occupied since 1565, St. Augustine was founded forty-two years before the colony at Jamestown and fifty-five years before the ocean-weary Pilgrims set foot on Plymouth Rock! A highly recommended movie, *Dream of Empire,* brings this dramatic story to life. The film is shown at the Visitors Center, 10 Castillo Drive, 9:00 A.M.–5:00 P.M. daily; (904) 824–0339 or (904) 825–1000.

Imposing ◆**Castillo de San Marcos** is well worth a visit. The King of Spain spent $30 million on this fort, which took nearly a quarter century to build. Overlooking Matanzas Bay, this national monument withstood many a siege but was never captured. Park rangers in Spanish uniforms provide plenty of smoke as well as action with their demonstrations of old-time firearms. Castillo de San Marcos National Monument, 1 Castillo Drive, St. Augustine. Open 8:45 A.M.–4:45 P.M.; (904) 829–6506.

A faithful reconstruction of the 1750–1845 period centers on ◆**St. George Street.** To absorb the Old World atmosphere, take a leisurely stroll by coquina-stone houses with overhanging balconies and walled garden patios that line the narrow streets. Be sure to visit the exquisite **St. Photios National Greek Orthodox Shrine** at 41 St. George Street. (Open 9:00 A.M.–5:00 P.M.) Attractive shops and restaurants lure visitors. You'll want to browse the **Ancient Mariner** gift shop and follow your nose to the **Spanish Bakery.** Ask for Spanish meat turnovers, better known as empanadas, to eat in the picnic area. (The bakery is open 9:00 A.M.–3:00 P.M.) The historic area is immediately south of the old city gate.

Don't miss the ◆ **Spanish Quarter** in the restoration area. Here the daily lives of soldiers and settlers are re-created by costumed guides and craftspeople who welcome your questions. Look for the red and white Spanish flag and enter at the **Triay Orientation Center** on St. George Street. Operated by the state, this quality attraction is open 9:00 A.M.–5:00 P.M. daily. Information and ticket window at the Triay House, St. George Street, St. Augustine; (904) 825–6830.

St. Augustine experienced its first tourism boom at the turn of the century, thanks to Henry Flagler. Impressed with the city's possibilities, he linked St. Augustine and Jacksonville by railroad. While he was at it, Flagler turned the town into a fashionable resort by building two grand hotels, the **Ponce de Leon** and the **Alcazar.** Visitors should not leave the city without at least a look at these two lavish hotels, their gardens, and fountains. The Ponce de Leon serves as **Flagler College** (no charge to roam the campus), and the restored Alcazar houses the ◆ **Lightner Museum** with its three floors of fascinating collections. Open 9:00 A.M.–5:00 P.M. daily; (904) 824–2874. Both are at Cordova and King streets, St. Augustine.

What better spot to lunch than in the indoor swimming pool (fortunately it was drained some time ago) of the fantastic Alcazar Hotel (now the Lightner Museum). ◆ **Cafe Alcazar** is located in the rear of the museum right in the center of the **Lightner Antique Mall.** You may investigate the antiques shops while waiting for a sandwich, salad, or freshly baked quiche. Appropriately, considering the grand setting, the dozen tables are set with real flowers, linen tablecloths, and china. Everything is tasty, especially the salad Alcazar and Alcazar ambrosia. Open 11:30 A.M.–2:30 P.M. Tuesday through Saturday and for brunch on Sunday 10:30 A.M.–2:00 P.M. Lunch prices are inexpensive; (904) 824–7813.

Imagine having dinner in your own private thatched hut overlooking the water at sunset. ◆ **The Conch House Restaurant** is known for succulent seafood as well as an enchanting tropical atmosphere. This unusual restaurant is the brainchild of the Ponces, who are descended from the Solanas, believed to be the oldest documented family in the United States. Family records on file in the Catholic Cathedral in St. Augustine date back to 1594.

The owners' interest in local history is evidenced in the extensive collection of nautical antiques used throughout the restaurant. The thatched roof, made of more than 8,000 palm fronds, is the work of the Ponce brothers and a Seminole Indian and his son.

The Conch House Restaurant steams its seafood entrees in special spices and sauces and offers as well grilled, broiled, and fried dishes. Specialties of the house include conch chowder, conch fritters, stuffed clams, and Captain Jim's Steamed Clams. Try the steamed seafood for two. Sensational!

You have your choice of dining on the outdoor deck, in a private dining pod, or inside the restaurant. Come by sea (free dockage while dining) or by land. After crossing the Bridge of Lions from the historic area of St. Augustine, take SR A1A South for 6 blocks, turn left at sign, go 2½ blocks to 57 Comares Avenue, St. Augustine. Open Sunday through Thursday 8:30 A.M.–9:00 P.M. and Friday and Saturday 8:30 A.M.–10:00 P.M. Most dinner entrees range from moderate to expensive; (904) 824–2046.

Those seeking a spot to spend the night that is as charming as

The Conch House Restaurant

it is convenient should make reservations at **The Kenwood Inn.** This bed-and-breakfast hostelry (built between 1865 and 1886) is located within the Historic District between the Oldest House and the famous Castillo de San Marcos. Most of St. Augustine's historic sights and fine restaurants are within walking distance.

The fifteen rooms range in size from small and cozy to spacious; each has its own unique personality (choose Shaker, colonial, or Victorian), and all have private baths. A small outdoor swimming pool is an appreciated extra, and innkeepers Mark and Kerrianne Constant make everyone (except small children and pets) feel warmly welcome. The Kenwood Inn, 38 Marine Street, St. Augustine, FL 32084; (904) 824–2116.

South of St. Augustine are sights in Bunnell and Palatka not to be missed. The ❖ **Bulow Plantation Ruins Historic Site** features an old sugar mill and the crumbling foundation of an ancient mansion destroyed during the Seminole Indian Wars. Guided tours are available on request. The ruins are southeast of Bunnell on Old Kings Road. Open 9:00 A.M.–5:00 P.M.; (904) 517–2084.

If your thoughts turn to ❖ **Palatka Ravine State Ornamental Garden,** it's probably spring. During February and March, the azaleas and camellias are at their peak. You may drive the road that loops around the edges of three steep ravines, jog the popular exercise course, or just stroll the paths thinking end-of-winter thoughts. One hundred thousand azaleas can't be wrong. A mile southeast of Palatka on Twigg Street (off Moseley Avenue); (904) 329–3721. Open daily 8:00 A.M. to sunset.

GAINESVILLE AREA

Marjorie Kinnan Rawlings found inspiration in the backwater community of Cross Creek. This semitropical low country was the setting for her Pulitzer Prize–winning novel, *The Yearling.* The author's rambling farmhouse, complete with old-fashioned canned goods on the kitchen shelves and her antique typewriter on the screened porch, looks as if she had just stepped out for a moment.

Rawlings quickly grew to love this place and its people, which she immortalized in her autobiographical book, *Cross Creek.* Her neighbors were "crackers," rural folk native to the region who were used to "making do." They made what living there was from the land, put on no airs, and wore their southern heritage with pride. The author compiled a book of regional recipes titled *Cross Creek Cookery*. The ❖**Marjorie Kinnan Rawlings State Historic Site** is in Cross Creek, off CR 325. Open Thursday through Sunday 10:00–11:30 A.M. and 1:00–3:30 P.M. Tours are given every hour from 10:00 A.M. to 4:00 P.M. (except noon). House closed August and September. Marjorie Kinnan Rawlings State Historic Site, Route 3, Box 92, Hawthorne, FL 32640; (904) 466–3672.

Florida's home where the buffalo roam is ❖**Payne's Prairie State Preserve** just south of Gainesville. Indian artifacts dating back to 7000 B.C. have been unearthed here. The visitor center contains interesting exhibits on the natural and cultural history of the preserve. (It was once a large Spanish cattle ranch.) A nearby observation tower provides a scenic overlook of this vast, marshy sea of grass.

The park offers boating (no gasoline-powered boats allowed) and fishing in Lake Wauberg, as well as camping, bird-watching, and horseback riding. (Bring your own horse.) The entrance is on U.S. 441, approximately 1½ miles north of Micanopy. Open 8:00 A.M. to sunset year-round. Payne's Prairie State Preserve, Route 2, Box 41, Micanopy, FL 32667; (904) 466–3397.

The **Wine and Cheese Gallery** in Gainesville, with umbrellaed tables in a shady courtyard, is a fine spot for lunching. Go right on through the front of the Gallery—which is a gourmet food and wine shop—and hang a left to reach the courtyard. In inclement weather, take a right to the inside dining room. As you might imagine, they offer a super selection of wines, or you may choose from more than a hundred kinds of imported beer. The sandwiches are a treat (they bake their own French bread), as are the salads. Try the Big Cheese, a fat sandwich consisting of Cream Havarti, Jarlsberg, and Gouda, or a lettuce salad loaded with rare roast beef, fresh mushrooms, and Jarlsberg. The Wine and Cheese Gallery is at 113 N. Main Street in Gainesville. Open 11:00 A.M.–2:15 P.M. Monday through Saturday; (904) 372–8446. Inexpensive to moderate.

Gainesville's outstanding ❖**Florida Museum of Natural History** offers fascination for all ages with its replica of a Mayan palace and reconstructed Florida cave. (The cave comes complete with cave critters, but don't worry, they don't fly.) What a find! The museum is on the University of Florida campus at the corner of Newell Drive and Museum Road. Open Monday through Saturday 10:00 A.M.–5:00 P.M. and Sunday and holidays 1:00–5:00 P.M. Admission and parking are free; call (904) 392–1721. The museum's Collectors Shop, open during museum hours, carries a fine selection of items relating to the natural and social sciences.

Just down the road from the museum is the lush **Lake Alice Wildlife Preserve,** home base for alligators that fit easily into the whopper category. Don't mess with them but do enjoy this lovely spot. The preserve is on Museum Road, a mile west of S.W. Thirteenth Street.

Some fossils that have shed light on Florida's ancient history were found 2 miles northwest of Gainesville at the ✤ **Devil's Millhopper State Geological Site.** This huge five-acre sinkhole has yielded shark teeth and other evidence of the prehistoric sea that once covered the state. Some of the plants and animals in the 120-foot-deep collapsed caverns are more typical of the Appalachian Mountains than of Florida. Off SR 232 (Millhopper Road). Devil's Millhopper State Geological Site, 4732 N.W. Fifty-third Avenue, Gainesville, FL 32601. Open 9:00 A.M.–5:00 P.M. October to the end of April; (904) 955–2008.

At ✤ **O'Leno State Park,** the scenic Sante Fe River performs a real disappearing act as it flows underground for more than 3 miles before coming to the surface. Other natural features of O'Leno are sinkholes, hardwood hammocks, river swamp, and sandhill communities. You'll find a good view of the river from the suspension bridge built by the Civilian Conservation Corps in the late 1930s. A fine place to camp, canoe, fish, swim, or walk the nature trails. The park is off U.S. 41, 25 miles northwest of Gainesville. Open 8:00 A.M. to sunset year-round. O'Leno State Park, Route 2, Box 1010, High Springs, FL 32643; (904) 454–1853.

✤ **Ichetucknee Springs State Park** features a pristine crystal-clear river, but it is not exactly undiscovered. Floating down the scenic Ichetucknee in an inner tube has become so popular the park limits tubers to protect vegetation. Spending a day (or a few hours) on this river is a perfectly splendid thing to do. The current moves you effortlessly along so you can enjoy the surrounding beauty. No wonder this is such a popular pastime.

The river's source is a group of springs that boil out of limestone sinks and trickle out from under cypress tree roots to the
tune of 233 million gallons a day. Ichetucknee is the state's third
largest spring, an impressive statistic in a state that claims more
springs than any other.
At the park entrance you will receive a map of tubing options.
No food, drink, tobacco, disposable items, or pets are allowed on
the river. The peak season is May through September when the
park is apt to be most crowded. At other times, you can occasionally have the river to yourself. The water is 72 degrees year-
round. Local vendors rent tubes and canoes. The park, which is
north of Gainesville, off I–75, and 4 miles northwest of Fort
White, off SR 47 and CR 238, is open 8:00 A.M. to sunset. For
maps and details, contact the north entrance of Ichetucknee State
Park on CR 238 or call (904) 497–2511. For recorded information call (904) 497–4690.

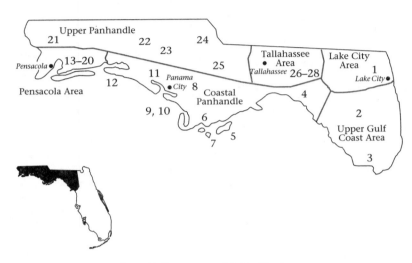

1. Stephen Foster State Folk Culture Center
2. Forest Capital State Museum
3. Cedar Key
4. St. Marks National Wildlife Refuge
5. St. George Island
6. John Gorrie Museum
7. St. Vincent National Wildlife Refuge
8. Dead Lakes State Recreation Area
9. St. Andrews
10. Shell Island
11. Eden State Gardens
12. Temple Mound Museum
13. Gulf Islands National Seashore
14. Fort Pickens
15. Seville Square
16. Pensacola Historical Museum
17. North Hill Preservation District
18. Hopkins' Boarding House
19. National Museum of Naval Aviation
20. Big Lagoon State Recreation Area
21. Blackwater River State Park
22. Lake DeFuniak
23. Falling Waters State Recreation Area
24. Florida Caverns State Park
25. Torreya State Park
26. Maclay Ornamental Gardens
27. Tallahassee Museum of Natural History and Science
28. Wakulla Springs

Northwest Florida

Lake City Area

The ◆ **Stephen Foster State Folk Culture Center** pays tribute to the man who made the Suwannee River famous, wrote "Old Folks at Home" (Florida's official state song), and gave us such long-standing favorites as "Oh Susannah" and "Camptown Races." One of America's best-loved composers, Stephen Foster was born in Pennsylvania in 1842 and died at the age of thirty-seven in New York City with 38 cents in his pocket. He never did get to see the Suwannee, but you should. It's the second-largest river in the state, and you may camp, boat, fish, and explore nature trails.

The **Foster Museum** is housed in an antebellum-style mansion that conjures up all sorts of romantic images of the Old South. The Carillon Tower chimes forth hourly concerts of Foster favorites. Inside you may take a trip through yesteryear as you inspect Foster memorabilia, antique musical instruments, original manuscripts, and animated dioramas.

The **Florida Folk Festival,** an annual gathering of folk musicians and craftspeople in May, is a well-attended event. The Jeanie Ball (named for "Jeanie with the Light Brown Hair") is the highlight of October, and December features popular Christmas Concerts. For a complete schedule of events, write Stephen Foster Center, P.O. Drawer G, White Springs, FL 32096; (904) 397-2733. The Stephen Foster Center is open every day 9:00 A.M.–5:00 P.M. White Springs is 3 miles east of I–75 and 10 miles northwest of Lake City at the junction of U.S. 41 and SR 136.

For another look at this well-known river, head west for **Suwannee River State Park.** The overlook above the confluence of the Suwannee and the Withlacoochee provides a commanding view of both rivers as well as a fine place for a picnic. Notice the remains of Confederate earthworks built to protect the railroad bridge across the Suwannee. Oaks bearded with moss and cypress trees canopy the tranquil river creating a scenic setting for those who enjoy camping, boating, fishing, and hiking. Open 8:00 A.M. to sunset. The park is 13 miles west of Live Oak off U.S. 90; (904) 362-2746.

UPPER GULF COAST

The ◆ **Forest Capital State Museum,** just south of Perry ("Tree Capital of the South"), pays tribute to forestry, the state's third-largest industry. This cypress geodesic dome features an old turpentine still as well as exhibits on such things as modern day turpentine production and the sex life of the pine tree. After learning about Florida's 314 known species of trees and the 5,000 products manufactured from the longleaf pine tree, take time to wander through the turn-of-the-century **Cracker Homestead** behind the visitor center. This log cabin home has a "dogtrot" (a breezeway), mosquito netting on the beds, and a kitchen that is separated from the house in case of fire. Near the well, tubs for washing clothes stand ready for action. (Keep in mind, these are the "good old days.") A grape arbor, outhouse, pantry house, chicken pen, barn, corncrib, cane grinder, and smokehouse round out the self-sufficient scene of yesteryear.

The Visitor Center Museum and Cracker Homestead are off U.S. 98-27A just south of Perry. The center is open 9:00 A.M.–5:00 P.M. (except noon–1:00 P.M.) every day except Tuesday and Wednesday and Thanksgiving, Christmas, and New Year's days. Forest Capital State Museum, 204 Forest Park Drive, Perry, FL 32347; (904) 584–3227.

In October the **Florida Forest Festival** celebrates by crowning a Forestry Queen and holding chain saw championships, arts and crafts shows, and the world's largest fish fry. For festival information call the Taylor County Chamber of Commerce, (904) 584–5366.

Halfway between Tallahassee and Tampa but a world apart from both, ◆ **Cedar Key** is far enough off the beaten interstate to have preserved the flavor of old Florida. (Take SR 24 off I–19 and 98.) This tiny fishing village is on the largest of more than a hundred islands clustered in the Gulf of Mexico. Three miles from the mainland, Cedar Key is officially on Way Key, which is connected to the mainland by causeway. Local restaurants, the beneficiaries of fishing, crabbing, scalloping, and oystering, are known for their sumptuous repasts.

Settled in the early 1840s, Cedar Key began to blossom in 1861 with the completion of Florida's first major railroad, which ran from Fernandina in the northeast corner of the state to Cedar

Key. This led to a boom in the lumber business and brought trainloads of tourists. It seems incredible today, but Cedar Key was once the second-largest city in Florida.

After the Civil War, Cedar Key developed a reputation as a center for shipbuilding and manufacturing of wooden pencils. When the cedar forests had all been leveled, residents turned to the sea for their living. For a brief time the manufacture of brushes and brooms from palmetto fiber created a flurry of business activity, but the discovery of plastics decisively ended that enterprise. As if it needed a final "blow," this once-bustling port was devastated by the hurricane of 1896, from which it never fully recovered.

All these ups and downs are carefully documented at two pleasant little museums. **Cedar Key State Museum** and the **Cedar Key Historical Society Museum.** The State Museum, on Museum Drive, is open 9:00 A.M.–5:00 P.M. except for Tuesday and Wednesday; (904) 543–5350. The Cedar Key Historical Society Museum, on the corner of Second and D streets, is open Monday through Friday 11:00 A.M.–4:00 P.M. and Sunday 1:00–4:00 P.M.

Cedar Key's **National Wildlife Refuge,** covering three islands, gives rattlesnakes the same preferential treatment as birds. Sea views are embellished by the pink flash of a rare roseate spoonbill, freewheeling frigates, and pelicans crashing into the Gulf in search of supper. The refuge is strictly an environmental study area and not open for visitor use. But bird-watchers who rent a boat and cruise near the islands will be well rewarded.

Festival followers flock to the Cedar Key **Sidewalk Arts Festival** in April and the **Seafood Festival** in mid-October. For information contact the Cedar Key Area Chamber of Commerce at Second Street and SR 24, or call (904) 543–5600.

COASTAL PANHANDLE

◆ **St. Marks National Wildlife Refuge** consists of 90,000 acres of national forests, water areas, and the coast on the Gulf of Mexico. Stop in the headquarters and visitors center for a look at the interpretive displays and an observation-deck view of the marsh. Then take the scenic drive to the **St. Marks Lighthouse,** one of the oldest in the Southeast. Constructed in 1831 from stones removed from old Fort San Marcos de Apalache, this lighthouse guides modern vessels with the same lens it used during the Civil War. If you are a bird-watcher or an alligator watcher, you will be in your glory. (You'll feel even more glorious if you remembered the bug repellent.) Hike miles of primitive walking trails, including a 42-mile section of the Florida National Scenic Trail, and enjoy a picnic lunch overlooking the water near the lighthouse. The visitors center, 3 miles south of U.S. 98 on Lighthouse Road, is open 8:15 A.M.–4:15 P.M. Monday through Friday and Saturday and Sunday 10:00 A.M.–5:00 P.M. You are welcome in the refuge anytime during daylight hours to picnic, launch a boat, crab, or fish. Call (904) 925-6121.

San Marcos de Apalache State Museum is also the site of a fort first built in 1679 by the Spaniards. The fort was held at various times by the British, Spanish, and Confederate forces. Its capture by General Andrew Jackson in 1818 was an important factor in the United States' acquisition of Florida the next year. The museum contains artifacts spanning the area's history from the Spanish occupation to the Civil War. A lovely trail winds through Confederate earthworks, climbs to the top of a powder magazine, follows crumbling fort walls along the banks of the Wakulla River, and ends at the original site of early Spanish fortifications where the Wakulla and St. Marks River merge. The museum is 24 miles south of Tallahassee on SR 363 in St. Marks. Open Thursday through Monday 9:00 A.M.–5:00 P.M. San Marcos de Apalache, Box 27, St. Marks, FL 32355; (904) 925-6216.

Right around the corner from the museum is **Posey's,** "The Home of the Topless Oyster." Try the topless oyster, smoked mullet, baked oysters with bacon and cheese, or boiled shrimp. A live band entertains Friday, Saturday, and Sunday nights. Posey's, on the road to the museum in St. Marks, is open year-round. Inexpensive. (904) 925-6172.

Folks from Tallahassee head to the coast for fresh seafood, and one of their favorite destinations is **Spring Creek Restaurant.** This family operation hides out under live oaks festooned with Spanish moss where, according to the menu, "fresh spring water merges with the Gulf, creating the finest seafood in the world." Spring Creek serves up generous portions of mullet, crab fingers, oysters, lobster, deviled crab, and grouper, to name just a few. The salad bar comes to the table so you can build you own. Spe-

Posey's "Home of the Topless Oyster"

cialties are cheese grits and homemade desserts such as chocolate peanut butter pie and coconut cream pie. You might want to take home a jar of their tasty salad dressing dry mix, which makes eighteen pints with the addition of your own buttermilk and mayonnaise. Take U.S. 363 (S. Monroe Street) south from Tallahassee and go west on U.S. 98 and south on CR 365 to the tiny community of Spring Creek. Open for lunch and dinner on weekends. Closed Monday and Tuesday. Prices are mostly in the moderate range; (904) 926–3751.

Once you've started, there's no stopping. Fresh seafood is a fun addiction. **Angelo's Seafood Restaurant**'s roomy wrap-around deck is just the place to relax in a rocking chair and have a cocktail while the sun sets over the river. Try the char-broiled mullet, the soft-shell crab, or the snapper throats and, for sure, their Greek salad. Each table is served a corked wine bottle full of dressing. Angelo's "over the water" restaurant is right by the bridge in Panacea. Owners Angelo and Arline Petrandis take a lot of pride in their handsome restaurant, which is open Friday and Saturday 4:30–11:00 P.M., Sunday noon–10:00 P.M., and 4:30–10:00 P.M. every other day but Tuesday. Prices are mostly moderate. Call (904) 984–5168.

You really shouldn't drive through Carrabelle without tipping your hat to the **world's smallest police station.** You can't miss it. It's a public phone booth right on the main drag with an American flag painted on it. Often the patrol car is parked beside it waiting for the next call. If so, why not wave? Carrabelle doesn't even remotely resemble the Naked City.

Another favorite local spot in Carrabelle is **Harry's Bar.** You may choose dim interior with cozy booths, TV, and pool table, or an umbrellaed table in the sunny courtyard. You might want to check out the rumor that Harry makes the best gyros (pronounced *year-o's*) north of Tarpon Springs. If you're into imported beer, you're in the right place. Open 9:00 A.M.–midnight Sunday through Thursday. Food is served from 4:00 P.M. Tuesday through Saturday. Harry's is on Marine Street in Carrabelle; (904) 697–9982.

A British fort once stood at the **Fort Gadsden State Historic Site.** Held for a time by Indians and runaway slaves, it was destroyed by American forces in 1816. In 1818 Andrew Jackson ordered the fort to be rebuilt, but today only a bare outline is visible. A miniature replica of Fort Gadsden, some British muskets, and Indian artifacts are on display in an open-sided interpretive center. You may picnic, go fishing and boating on the Apalachicola River, and explore the nature trails. A short walk will take you to the remains of the renegade cemetery where grave robbers left nothing but shallow depressions. Fort Gadsden is 24 miles north of U.S. 98 just off SR 65 (21 miles of good road, the last 3 miles are rough) or 6 miles south of Sumatra off SR 65. Open daily 8:00 A.M. to sunset; (904) 643–2282. Free.

If you love the beach—the sand, the sea, and the sky—uncluttered by honky-tonk attractions, head for ◆ **St. George Island** at the end of Apalachicola Bay. The miles of underdeveloped beaches, sand dunes, and marshland are not totally wild. You'll find nature trails, boardwalks, observation platforms, picnic and camping areas, and bathhouses. Take the turnoff from U.S. 98 that leads across the toll bridge to St. George Island. Open daily 8:00 A.M. to sunset; (904) 927–2111.

Apalachicola's **Trinity Church,** one of the oldest (1830s) in the state, was cut in sections in New York and floated by schooner down the Atlantic Coast and around the Florida Keys. The original church bell was melted down to make Confederate cannon. Trinity, sometimes called the nation's first prefabricated church, is on Sixth Street, a block off U.S. 98, across from the Gorrie Museum in Apalachicola; (904) 653–9550. Free.

Whether you know it or not, you owe a lot to John Gorrie. He's the physician whose inventions make it possible for you to enjoy air-conditioning, refrigeration, and ice cubes in your drink. Back in the days when ice had to be shipped all the way from the Great Lakes, it was a precious commodity in Florida. Dr. John Gorrie wanted a way to cool the rooms of patients suffering from malaria. The only problem was that the pipes in his experimental machine kept clogging with ice. When he realized the importance of this accidental discovery, he immediately built a small ice-making machine. You may inspect a replica of the machine (patented in 1851) that paved the way for modern refrigeration and air-conditioning in the ◆**John Gorrie Museum.** (The original machine is in the Smithsonian Institution.) This one-room museum also has displays on cotton, lumbering, fishing, and other aspects of early Apalachicola history. The museum is at Avenue C and Sixth Street, 1 block off U.S. 319-98 in Apalachicola. Open 9:00 A.M.–5:00 P.M. daily except Tuesday and Wednesday; (904) 653–9347.

◆**St. Vincent National Wildlife Refuge** on St. Vincent Island is a bridgeless gem given over to some interesting animals and birds. White-tailed deer, wild hogs, raccoons, and opossums share the triangular-shaped refuge with sambar deer, which were imported from India by early owners. Red-tailed hawks, peregrine falcons, bald eagles, and a host of songbirds and waterfowl come and go. The deserted beaches are a favorite nesting ground for sea turtles. Most alligators hang around the freshwater ponds and marshes, while a few individualists choose to sun on the beach and enjoy the surf. Something to remember when taking a swim! This splendid place, with mile after mile of unspoiled beach, can be reached only by water. Contact the refuge manager for information on freshwater fishing, island exploration, and the cost of managed hunts for deer and wild hog. No charge for using the island, but you'll have to make your own arrangements to get there. Refuge Manager, St. Vincent National Wildlife Refuge, P.O. Box 447, Apalachicola, FL 32329; (904) 653–8808.

If you would like to see where the first of Florida's five constitutions was written, stop in at the **Constitution Convention State Museum.** Here you'll view an impressive replica of the Convention Hall's west wing, see eighteenth-century artifacts, and learn the story of the town of St. Joseph, which vanished forever after the 1844 hurricane. The museum is a quarter mile east of U.S. 98, just south of Port St. Joe. Open Thursday through Monday 9:00 A.M.–noon and 1:00–5:00 P.M.; (904) 229–8029.

Strange as it may seem, the Dead Lakes are alive with fish. Named for thousands of cypress, oak, and pine trees that drowned in the natural overflow of the Chipola River, ✦ **Dead Lakes State Recreation Area** enjoys a reputation as one of the best freshwater fishing spots in the Florida Panhandle. A longleaf pine forest shelters a tranquil picnic and camping area, and large stands of bare trees create a place of haunting beauty. One mile north of Wewahitchka on SR 71. Open 8:00 A.M. to sunset year-round. Dead Lakes State Recreation Area, P.O. Box 989, Wewahitchka, FL 32465; (904) 639–2702.

Another state recreation area that takes advantage of the Panhandle's gloriously white beaches is ✦ **St. Andrews** near Panama City. The water is unusually clear, the dunes are picturesque, and the pine woods shade fine campsites. Be sure to take a look at the restored old-time "cracker" turpentine still. St. Andrews is 3 miles east of Panama City Beach on SR 392, 4607 State Park Lane, Panama City, FL 32408. Open 8:00 A.M. to sunset; (904) 233–5140.

One of the most popular boat trips along the Panhandle Gulf Coast is to ✦ **Shell Island.** This undeveloped treasure of long, white beaches and windswept dunes is perfect for barefoot beachcombers and those who enjoy long, uninterrupted views of the Gulf between swims. Seven and a half miles long and more than a mile wide, this pristine island boasts a freshwater lake and teems with wildlife. From St. Andrews State Park, boats leave four times daily for the western end of the island. Shell Island trips leave for the eastern end of the island from Captain Anderson's Marina on Thomas Drive at Grand Lagoon in Panama City. Boats make the trip twice daily from mid-May to mid-September at 9:00 A.M. and noon. Inquire about sightseeing and dinner cruises.

Call (904) 234–3435. From **Treasure Island Marina** at Grand Lagoon on Panama City Beach, a glass-bottom boat departs daily during the summer for a three-hour adventure called "Sea School." You will see dolphins, examine the contents of a shrimp net, and feed birds. Recorded message: (904) 234–8944. Treasure Island Marina: (904) 234–6533.

Farther up the coast, the landscaped grounds and mansion of ❖ **Eden State Gardens** overlook Choctawhatchee Bay. Once the hub of a large sawmill complex, the lumber baron's antebellum residence now stands alone framed by gnarled oaks dripping with Spanish moss. The stately white-columned mansion with a fireplace in every room preserves a fragment of the 1800s, the Old South that has mostly gone with the wind. You may picnic, fish, and take a guided tour of this splendid house. Five miles north of Grayton Beach, Eden State Gardens is on CR 395, 1 mile off U.S. 98 in Point Washington. Tours of the house are offered Thursday through Monday on the hour, 9:00 A.M.–4:00 P.M., and the park is open daily 8:00 A.M. to sunset. Eden State Gardens, P.O. Box 26, Point Washington, FL 32454; (904) 231–4214.

Few places are prettier than **Grayton Beach State Recreation Area** with its blue-green waters and white-white sand dunes crested by dense stands of sea oats. Artists come here to capture the beauty of trees stunted and sculpted by wind and salt spray. Swimming and camping are popular, of course, and this is a fine place to fish—either in the surf or in the brackish waters of Western Lake. About 25 miles east of Fort Walton Beach by way of U.S. 98 and SR 30A. Grayton State Recreation Area, 357 Main Park Road, Santa Rosa Beach, FL 32459; (904) 231–4210.

Rocky Bayou State Recreation Area provides an opportunity to see what the real Florida looks like. Located within Eglin Air Force Base, this park sits on the arm of Choctawhatchee Bay known as Rocky Bayou. A freshwater lake by the unlikely name of Puddin Head is home to largemouth bass, alligators, and a colony of beavers, and nature trails wind through a sand forest shading reindeer moss and scrub oaks. The area is good for camping, swimming, boating, and fishing. Open 8:00 A.M. to sunset; located 3 miles east of Niceville off Highway 20. Fred Gannon Rocky Bayou State Recreation Area, 4281 Highway 20, Niceville, FL 32578; (904) 833–9144.

How do you like your mullet—smoked, baked, broiled, fried, or in gumbo? The great thing about the **Boggy Bayou Mullet Festival** is that you don't have to decide—you can try it every which way. In the early 1900s mullet was a very important food source as well as the primary livelihood for most of the settlers who lived in this area. Mullet were caught, salted, and shipped by boat first to Pensacola, then to other communities in the South. Of course, the festival offers plenty of other tempting things to eat, including specialties from many foreign lands, and you can feast your eyes on the Queen of the Mullet Festival Pageant. The Boggy Bayou Mullet Festival is held the third weekend in October at College Boulevard and Highway 85 north of Niceville. The festival address is P.O. Box 231, Niceville, FL 32588. Admission, parking, and nonstop professional entertainment are all free. (904) 678–1615.

Local history takes on new meaning at the **Heritage Museum** in Valparaiso. Besides an extensive library of old documents and maps (including *The Complete and Official Records of the Union and Confederate Armies*), the museum houses a collection of artifacts that provides insight into the challenges faced by prehistoric Indians and early pioneers. You'll want to inspect the steam-powered cotton gin as well as tools used in farming, lumbering, and producing turpentine. Classes are offered in weaving, quilt-making, needlepoint, tatting, and basket-weaving, and hand-crafted items are for sale. The Heritage Museum is at 115 Westview Avenue in downtown Valparaiso. Open Tuesday through Saturday 11:00 A.M.–4:00 P.M.; (904) 678–2615. Free.

The **Air Force Armament Museum** is outside the west gate of Eglin Air Force Base, the largest air force base in the free world. The awesome SR–71 Blackbird spy plane and other military aircraft outside compete with interior displays and ongoing movies. The Desert Storm section brings you up to the minute weapon-wise. Eglin Air Force Base is 13 miles northeast of Fort Walton Beach. For information call (904) 882–4062.

The historic fishing village of Destin was founded in the 1830s when Captain Leonard A. Destin sailed into Choctawhatchee Bay and decided it was a fine place to raise his family. The two-room **Old Destin Post Office Museum** is full of artifacts and photos that tell of the early days of this community. If you want to know more about life in "Old Destin," a short history of the village titled ". . . And the Roots Run Deep" is for sale. The staff may be able to help with genealogical research on early Destin families. The museum is on Stahlman Avenue, across from the Destin Library in Destin. Open Wednesdays 1:30–4:30 P.M. Old Destin Post Office Museum, P.O. Box 691, Destin, FL 32540–0691. No admission fee and no charge for guided tour. (904) 837–8572.

In 1933 the isolated fishing village of Destin underwent a dramatic change. A wooden bridge was built connecting it to the outside world. Before long, folks began to notice Destin was not only the "luckiest fishing village" but also had some of the finest beaches anywhere. From red snapper to yellowfin tuna, an abundance of incredibly fresh and delectable seafood lands in area restaurants. Emerald Coast favorites include **Marina Cafe,** whose gifted young chef dresses grilled grouper with Louisiana crawfish tails and sauce meunière. For lunch, savor a seafood combo at **Fudpuckers;** a juicy burger at **Harry T's Boathouse,** where circus memorabilia includes Stretch, Harry's beloved (stuffed!) giraffe; or the superb char-grilled amberjack sandwich, served with a side-order view of parasailors and other assorted beach action, at the **BackPorch** on Old Highway 98.

Indians were dining on fresh seafood long before the Europeans "discovered" Florida. Some of them were mound builders, and they left a fine example of their work on the main drag in **Fort Walton Beach.** Imagine 500,000 basketloads of dirt hauled one at a time to create this impressive landmark. To learn more about the seven pre-Columbian cultures who inhabited this area for more than 10,000 years, drop in at the Indian ◆ **Temple Mound Museum** on the east flank of the mound. Here you'll see the re-creation of an ancient temple, a four-legged bowl that has been called the most unique ceramic artifact in the Southeast, and various artifacts from recent archaeological excavations.

The museum and mound (which is a National Historic Landmark), at 139 Miracle Strip Parkway on U.S. 98, are owned and operated by the City of Fort Walton Beach. The mound may be viewed during daylight hours. The museum is open 11:00 A.M.–4:00 P.M. Monday through Friday and 9:00 A.M.–4:00 P.M. Saturday, September to May. (904) 243–6521.

Once upon a time a buccaneer known as Billy Bowlegs decided

being a run-of-the-mill pirate wasn't classy enough, so he assembled a group of followers—Indians, deserters, bandits, and the like—and proclaimed himself King of Florida. He did all the things pirates were supposed to do—scared folks out of their wits, took their money and buried it, and, in general, made a nuisance of himself. For more than thirty years Fort Walton Beach has been annually reviving his swashbuckling spirit in the rollicking **Billy Bowlegs Festival.** The first week in June erupts in mock pirate attacks, parades, concerts, ski shows, boat races, crafts exhibits, and, of course, treasure hunts. For information write Greater Fort Walton Beach Chamber of Commerce, P.O. Box 640, Fort Walton Beach, FL 32549; (904) 244–8191.

PENSACOLA AREA

Beach lovers can rest easy. ✪ **Gulf Islands National Seashore** protects shimmering white sand and swaying sea oats along a 150-mile stretch of islands and keys between Destin, Florida, and Gulfport, Mississippi. The Florida section of the national seashore includes **Naval Live Oaks Area** (where you may hike through groves once prized for shipbuilding), part of **Perdido Key,** the forts on the **Pensacola Naval Air Station,** and part of **Santa Rosa Island.**

At the western end of Santa Rosa is stabilized, historic ✪ **Fort Pickens,** which saw action during the Civil War and where Apache chief Geronimo was held prisoner for two ignominious years. Today the beach gets better use as a bird sanctuary and camping and recreation site. Ask the park rangers or local dive ships to recommend the best scuba diving locations. Besides the usual beach activities, you'll want to explore this massive five-sided fort and visit the small museum. Take U.S. 98 and SR 399 south to Pensacola Beach, then follow signs west to Fort Pickens. Museum open 9:30 A.M.–5:00 P.M. daily April through October and 8:30 A.M.–4:00 P.M. November through March. For information: Superintendent, Gulf Islands National Seashore, 1801 Gulf Breeze Parkway, Gulf Breeze, FL 32561; (904) 934–2600.

Fisherfolk should not miss the opportunity to drop a line from the **"world's longest fishing pier,"** as the old Pensacola Bay Bridge is now known. Judging from the number of fishing poles sprouting from the bridge, this is one hot spot. And no through traffic interferes with your concentration. Easy to find, this bridge parallels the new Pensacola Bay Bridge.

The heart of Pensacola is in ❖ **Seville Square,** a historic district between E. Government and S. Alcaniz streets where shops, restaurants, museums, and art galleries inhabit a hodgepodge of restored eighteenth- and nineteenth-century cottages and mansions. Pick up a free map and brochures at the Visitor Information Center, 1401 E. Gregory Street (at the foot of the bridge), Pensacola, FL 32501; (800) 874–1234 or (904) 434–1234.

Stop in at the ❖ **Pensacola Historical Museum** in Old Christ Church, the oldest church building still standing in the state. Once used by the Union Army as a barracks and hospital, the church now is a repository of local history including everything from displays on ancient Indian culture and Mardi Gras costumes to a fully equipped 1915 kitchen. Located at 405 S. Adams Street and Zaragoza Street, Pensacola, FL; (904) 433–1559. Open Monday through Saturday 9:00 A.M.–4:30 P.M.

For a delightful glimpse into Pensacola's past, browse the **Museums of Industry and Commerce,** chat with costumed interpreters in five different house museums, and shop a wide variety of attractive boutiques in **Historic Pensacola Village.** Don't miss the truly weird collection (including both shrunken heads and a petrified cat) in the newly renovated **T. T. Wentworth, Jr., Florida State Museum.** Kids love **Discovery!,** the lively hands-on children's museum upstairs.

Hungry? Try **McGuires,** one of Pensacola's favorite watering holes. The fare is top-notch, the portions generous, and the atmosphere, well, loaded. Thirty thousand one-dollar bills adorn the walls from which stuffed hippos, moose, and cape buffalo stare. Prices are reasonable, unless (lottery winners take note!) you're hankering for a McGuires famous $100 burger. You might want to try **Skopelos on the Bay Seafood and Steak Restaurant** or **Jamie's French Restaurant** in a nineteenth-century cottage in historic Seville Square. A favorite beach eatery is **Jubilee Restaurant and Oyster Bar** with quick, casual meals on the lower level and elegant Florida cuisine upstairs.

Not to be missed is **Seville Quarter** with **Rosie O'Grady's Good Time Emporium** and seven other saloons and restaurants. Even if you're not hungry, thirsty, or in need of entertainment, you really should stop in for a look. Besides an impressive collection of local antiques, the gaslights are from Liverpool, the parliament benches are from London, the disco booth was once an English pulpit, the ships' wheels in Coppersmith's Gallery are from schooners that made tea and spice runs to China, and Rosie's main door at one time graced a mansion in Mobile.

Seville Quarter overflows with choices. Should you down a Flaming Hurricane drink at Rosie's, catch the show on big screen TV in **Lili Marlene's World War I Aviators Pub,** or tap your feet to **Apple Annie's** wonderful bluegrass music? While you're deciding, you might want to order red beans and rice, jambalaya, or beignet doughnuts in the **Palace Oyster Bar.** For an inexpensive lunch, choose oysters on the half shell or a Cajun sausage sandwich. Those great pub mirrors on the walls were imported from Edinburgh, Scotland. The Seville Quarter is at 130 E. Government Street in Pensacola, and the prices range from inexpensive to expensive. (904) 434–6211.

Take a ride, or better yet a walk, through ◆**North Hill Preservation District.** This 50-block area, bounded by LaRua, Palafox, Blount, and Reus streets, is a treasure trove of fancy turn-of-the-century houses. You'll be able to appreciate the details—the wide verandas, turrets, and elaborate gingerbread trim—better on foot. Maps and touring information are free from the Visitor Information Center (open 8:30 A.M.–5:00 P.M.), 1401 E. Gregory Street, at the foot of Pensacola Bay Bridge.

All your roaming through the North Hill Preservation District is sure to give you a stupendous appetite. You'll need it if you try to do justice to the good southern cooking at ◆**Hopkins' Boarding House.** This bustling establishment is the real thing, an authentic boarding house where you join other diners at big round tables and get to try out your boarding house reach. The place is usually pretty packed, and you may have to wait a few moments to be seated. If so, just grab a rocking chair on the wraparound porch and think ravenous thoughts.

Most first-timers are overwhelmed by the great steaming bowls of food that are replaced before they are emptied. A recent offering included fried chicken, rice, gravy, cole slaw, potato salad, corn muffins, black-eyed peas, cucumber salad, greens, succotash, macaroni and cheese, cake, jello, and lots of ice tea. Before you get so stuffed you can hardly see, take a look around at the religious pictures, collections of plates, and family photographs that adorn the walls.

You are expected to clear your own plate and to pay cash. Hopkins' Boarding House is at 900 N. Spring Street in the North Hill Preservation District of Pensacola. Opens at 11:00 A.M. Tuesday through Saturday for lunch and 5:00–7:30 P.M. for dinner. Closed Mondays. Inexpensive. (904) 438–3979.

The expansive ✪ **National Museum of Naval Aviation** is a real prize—a beautifully designed, fascinating tribute to aviation history on the grounds of the world's largest naval air station. You'll follow the growth and development of our country's naval aviation from the first aircraft the Navy purchased in 1911 (replica) to the Skylab command module. Especially fascinating is the movie of the inspiring *Great Flight,* the first successful crossing of the Atlantic Ocean by air in 1919. The only museum in the world devoted exclusively to naval aviation, this one has something for everyone. You can try out the controls of a jet trainer, wander among full-size aircraft, or browse the bookstore and gift shop. An impressive new wing features a dramatic seven-story atrium with four full-size Blue Angel sky hawks soaring in permanent diamond formation. Use the main entrance of the Naval Air Station. In Pensacola take Palafox Street south to Garden Street, which becomes Navy Boulevard (SR 295). Follow the signs to the Naval Air Station; (904) 452–3604. Open 9:00 A.M.–5:00 P.M. Closed Thanksgiving, Christmas, and New Year's days. A real bargain, it's free.

The **Naval Air Station** features a number of other attractions visitors sometimes miss because they simply don't realize they are so close by. The **Spanish Fort San Carlos de Barrancas** (part of the Gulf Islands National Seashore) is practically across the road from the museum. First, stop in the visitor center to get some background information, then explore the fort and enjoy its commanding view. Be careful in the dark, steep, and sometimes slippery tunnel to the water battery.

You can't enter the **Old Pensacola Lighthouse,** but as you drive by it's nice to know it has been operating since 1825. You will also want to take a look at **Sherman Field,** home of the famous precision flying team known as the Blue Angels. The Pensacola Naval Air Station main entrance is on Navy Boulevard, SR 295. Free.

While you're in the area, take advantage of the fine facilities at ◆ **Big Lagoon State Recreation Area** where you may picnic, camp, boat, fish, and swim. An elaborate boardwalk network and observation tower at East Beach provide bird-watchers with an excellent view overlooking the marsh. This is definitely the place to watch the great blue heron stalking his dinner! Also, you may soak up panoramic vistas of Big Lagoon, the park, and Gulf Islands National Seashore across the Intracoastal Waterway. The park is about 10 miles southwest of Pensacola off SR 292. Big Lagoon State Recreation Area, 12301 Gulf Beach Highway, Pensacola, FL 32507; (904) 492–1595.

UPPER PANHANDLE

Canoeists and campers will appreciate ◆ **Blackwater River State Park** on the shores of one of the cleanest rivers in the country. Dark water contrasts with dazzling white sandbars at bends in the river. Especially good for novice paddlers, the river winds its way from Alabama to Blackwater Bay at the leisurely rate of 3 to 4 mph. The park is 15 miles northeast of Milton, 3 miles off U.S. 90. Blackwater River State Park, 7720 Deaton Bridge Road, Holt, FL 32564; (904) 623–2363.

Put on your hiking shoes and heed the call of the **Jackson Red Ground Hiking Trail.** Located in Blackwater River State Forest, this old 21-mile Indian trading trail was used by Gen. Andrew Jackson on his historic 1818 journey to the Florida Territory. Follow the red paint marks on trees from Karick Lake to the Red Rock Picnic Area over a combination of footpaths and forest roadways.

The Jackson Trail, which is part of the National Recreation Trail System and designated as a section of the Florida Trail System, has a camping shelter. For information weekdays 7:00 A.M.–4:00 P.M., contact Blackwater Forestry Center, 11650 Munson Highway, Milton, FL 32570; (904) 957–4201. At other times park rangers are available at the Krul Recreation Area and the Coldwater Recreation Area.

What if you are overcome by a craving for pizza and you happen to be in Crestview, Florida? Consider yourself lucky and head on down to the **Hideaway** on Main Street. The dough is made from scratch twice daily, the sausage is cut, ground, and seasoned on the premises, and the sauce, according to a special recipe, is made fresh every morning. The Hideaway takes pride in not using any artificial emulsifiers or preservatives; its salad bar is crispy fresh, and a glass partition gives you a view of its immaculate kitchen. The Hideaway is at 326 N. Main Street in Crestview. Open Monday through Thursday 11:00 A.M.–9:00 P.M., Friday and Saturday 11:00 A.M.–10:00 P.M., closed Sunday. To order ahead or place a take-out order, call (904) 682–3225. Inexpensive.

⬥ **Lake DeFuniak,** halfway between Pensacola and Tallahassee, is well worth a visit. For one thing, this claims to be one of two perfectly round lakes in the world, and, for another, the area has a rich and fascinating heritage. During the 1880s a railroad executive envisioned a splendid winter resort here. Later, the Chautauqua Committee decided this would make a fine winter site for its program of concerts and lectures given each summer at Lake Chautauqua, New York. Take some time to admire the late nineteenth-century **Chautauqua Assembly Building** and the grand, old homes that surround the lake. The U.S. Department of the Interior and the National Parks Service recently placed the **Town of DeFuniak Springs** on the National Register of Historic Districts, citing some 285 structures of significant historic value. The Great Depression ended this glorious era, but an annual festival helps preserve memories of the past. The lake is in DeFuniak Springs near U.S. 90 and SR 83. For information on the festival held each year in April, call the Walton County Chamber of Commerce; (904) 892–3191.

Don't miss seeing one of the town's most historically significant structures, the **Walton-DeFuniak Public Library.** Opened on December 20, 1887, this is believed to be the state's oldest public library continuously operating in its original building. Its one room measured 24 by 17 feet and cost just under $580 when built. This charming library holds 20,000 volumes, including some rare books as old as the library itself.

You really wouldn't expect to find a fine European armor collection in such a modest little library, but that is one of the bonuses of getting off the beaten path. When Wallace Bruce was ambassador to Scotland and living in Edinburgh in the 1880s, his son Kenneth began collecting armor. The family came to DeFuniak Springs about 1890 when Mr. Bruce became president of the Chautauqua winter program. Some of the pieces of this unusual collection date back as far as the Crusades (1100–1300). Besides European pieces there are Kentucky rifles from the Daniel Boone era.

The entire collection was willed to Palmer College, but when the college closed in the 1930s, it was given to the city in partial payment of its debts. The city had no suitable place for it, so it eventually wound up in the library for you to enjoy. You won't have any trouble finding the library. Just drive around Lake DeFuniak and look for a tiny building. Closed Thursday and Sunday. The library's phone number is (904) 892–3624.

Walton-DeFuniak Public Library

Waterfalls in Florida? Strange as it may seem, they do exist in ◆ **Falling Waters State Recreation Area.** Though they don't exactly create a neck-craning Niagara, these waters do, just the same, fall. You see, some of the most notable geological features in Florida are its sinkholes. A small stream meanders into a 100-foot sinkhole, and *voilà*, a "waterfall!" A few caveats—you will be looking down, not up, and during the dry season there may not be any water to fall.

Not to worry. This forested area, the site of the first attempt (1919) to find oil in Florida, is lovely to stroll through. Limestone sinkholes honeycombing the hilly terrain may be viewed from a series of boardwalks. Take the self-guiding nature trails, picnic, camp, and swim. Located 3 miles south of Chipley, off SR 77A, the area is open 8:00 A.M. to sunset year-round. Falling Waters State Recreation Area, Route 5, Box 660, Chipley, FL 32428; (904) 638–6130.

Florida's caverns are another feature to come under the heading of strange quirks of geology. Over the millennium, mineral-rich drops of water have created the enchanting formations in ◆ **Florida Caverns State Park.** Among other sights, you'll see the **Waterfall Room,** the **Cathedral Room,** and the **Wedding Room**—all decked out in natural splendor. The caverns are as impressive, if not as large, as some of the country's most famous underground attractions. An enlightening audio-visual show in the visitor center explains how the caverns were formed, and exhibits on natural and cultural history shed some light on the early Indians who found shelter here.

The park also has a disappearing river, a natural bridge, and a white sand beach rimming Blue Hole Springs. You may camp, swim, fish, canoe, and picnic. The park, off SR 166, is 3 miles north of Marianna. Open 8:00 A.M. to sunset. Florida Caverns State Park, Marianna, FL 32446. Recorded message: (904) 482–9598. Office: (904) 482–1228.

If New England and Canada seem a trifle far to go for fall color, try ◆ **Torreya State Park.** Here rugged bluffs and ravines forested by flowers and hardwoods common to the North Georgia Appalachians provide the state's prettiest autumn display. The park, known as a botanist's paradise, protects the Torreya tree, which is native only to the 20-mile surrounding area. Be sure to tour the restored **Gregory Mansion** (1849), once home of an affluent cotton planter, and hike the trails to the Apalachicola River. The park, on SR 271 (which is off SR 12) between Bristol and Greensboro, is open 8:00 A.M. to sunset year-round. Guided tours of the house are given during the week at 10:00 A.M. and on weekends and holidays at 10:00 A.M., 2:00 P.M., and 4:00 P.M. Torreya State Park, Route 2, Box 70, Bristol, FL 32321; (904) 643–2674.

The fishing is fine at **Three Rivers State Recreation Area.** Named for the Chattahoochee and Flint rivers, which merge to form the Apalachicola, this scenic area includes 4 miles of shoreline on Lake Seminole at the Florida-Georgia border. Home to a slew of alligators and huge alligator snapping turtles as well as fish, Three Rivers is the place to wet a line, boat, picnic, or camp. Located a mile north of Sneads off SR 271, it's open 8:00 A.M. to sunset year-round. Three Rivers State Recreation Area, 7908 Three Rivers State Park Road, Sneads, FL 32460; (904) 482–9006.

TALLAHASSEE AREA

At the ✦**Maclay Ornamental Gardens** near Tallahassee, the peak blooming season begins in December and continues through April when dogwood, redbud, and more than a hundred varieties of camellias and azaleas create a fairyland of flowers. The gardens are an oasis of beauty all year, but spring is spectacular! This 307-acre park was once the home of Alfred B. Maclay, a New York financier who made his winter home here starting in 1923.

He developed the grounds as a hobby, using exotic plants to complement the native varieties and adding reflecting pools and avenues of stately palms. Stroll the brick walkways to the tiny walled garden where a graceful fountain provides the only sound except for the distant coo of the doves. If it's serenity you're after, you've come to the right place. Picnic grounds overlook Lake Hall, which is fine for swimming and boating (only electric motors allowed).

The park is open daily 8:00 A.M. to sundown year-round. The gardens and the **Maclay House Museum** are open daily 9:00 A.M.–5:00 P.M. January through April. The Maclay Gardens are 5 miles north of Tallahassee on U.S. 319. Alfred B. Maclay State Gardens, 3540 Thomasville Road, Tallahassee, FL 32308; (904) 487–4556 or (904) 487–4115.

The tradition of wintering in Florida was apparently started by Hernando de Soto in 1539. He and his men celebrated Christmas mass in the vicinity of **Lake Jackson Mounds State Archaeological Site** in what is believed to have been the first Christmas in the New World. That doesn't seem like such a long time ago when you consider that, on the basis of recent excavations, archaeologists now speculate the area was inhabited as early as 1,300 years before Christ.

The dominant features of this state park are impressive pyramid-shaped mounds that are the remains of the largest known Indian ceremonial center in north Florida. A way of life flourished here from A.D. 1300 to 1600 that revolved around a village, six temple mounds, and a burial mound. The Indians who lived here were farmers who traded their surplus crops with nearby villages. After you climb to the top of the highest mound, you will more fully appreciate the fact that these mounds were created by Indians carrying sand and clay, one basketful at a time! This is a lovely spot for a picnic and a walk through the woods. The Butler Mill Trail through a hardwood ravine and upland pine woods leads to an early 1880s gristmill site. The mounds are located 6 miles north of Tallahassee off U.S. 27 and are free. Call Lake Jackson Park Service at (904) 922–6007.

For more information about ancient Florida—its ice age, huge mastodons, resourceful Indians, and Spanish explorers—stop in at the **Museum of Florida History** in downtown Tallahassee. This is the place to learn abut Florida's role on the high seas, to inspect a pre–Civil War dugout boat, and to view precious gold doubloons. Florida's wild booms and busts, complete with a colorful cast of characters from pirates to lumber tycoons, are all part of the story. Fascinating for all ages, the museum is housed in the R. A. Grey Building (500 S. Bronough) across from the state Supreme Court in Tallahassee. Open every day but Christmas and Thanksgiving, 9:00 A.M.–4:30 P.M. Monday through Friday, 10:00 A.M.–4:30 P.M. Saturday, and noon–4:30 P.M. Sunday. No admission fee; (904) 488–1484.

The **LeMoyne Art Center and Sculpture Garden** is an oasis of peaceful beauty tucked into the middle of Tallahassee. The area's leading artists are represented in this compact gallery. A few metal sculptures adorn a small but lovingly cared for garden behind the gallery. For information write to LeMoyne Art Foundation, Inc., 125 N. Gadsen Street, Tallahassee, FL 32301. Open Tuesday through Saturday 10:00 A.M.–5:00 P.M., Sunday 1:00–5:00 P.M., closed holidays; (904) 222–8800 or 224–2714. Free.

The **Florida State Flying High Circus** serves up excitement the first two weekends in April. Students perform under the Big Top at Florida State University at W. Pensacola Street and Chieftain Way. Performances are Friday and Saturday at 7:00 P.M. with a matinee at 2:00 on Saturday afternoon. For details call (904) 644–4874. Campus tours and maps are available at the Visitor Information Center at 100 S. Woodward Street in Tallahassee; (904) 644–3246.

The ❖ **Tallahassee Museum of Natural History and Science** is a favorite haunt for adults as well as children who are curious about the way things were. At this authentic 1890 pioneer farm and community, you'll see demonstrations of blacksmithing, syrup making, sheep shearing, spinning, and weaving during the month of December. There are nature trails, exhibits of wild animals native to the area, a one-room schoolhouse, a gristmill, and the Bellevue Plantation, once the home of Prince and Princess Murat. The museum is at 3945 Museum Drive on Lake Bradford bordering Apalachicola National Forest. Open Monday through Saturday 10:00 A.M.–4:30 P.M. and Sunday 12:30–4:30 P.M.; (904) 488–1673.

If you'd like to peer into the world's deepest spring, head south of Tallahassee to ❖ **Wakulla Springs,** where limestone-filtered water gushes forth at more than 600,000 gallons per minute. Wakulla has been a sanctuary for wildlife and people ever since Indians fished its 185-foot depths and Spanish explorers refreshed themselves in its clean, clear waters. Tourists after the Civil War thought the springs well worth the trip, as did underwater filmmakers, who came as early as the mid-1940s.

The resort still has an old-fashioned flavor due to its emphasis on conservation rather than razzle-dazzle tourism. This 2,888-acre wildlife sanctuary provides a glorious glimpse into precondominium Florida. Jungle cruises and glass-bottom boat tours reveal an enchanting blend of scenery and wildlife. You'll see lots of alligators and elegant birds including snowy egrets, herons, and ibis.

One common meaning given for the Indian word *wakulla* is "mysteries of strange waters." The spring has its share of mysteries, including complete mastodon skeletons, which have been found in the bottom of the spring. It seems appropriate that this was the location for the filming of *Creature from the Black Lagoon.* After exploring the nature trails or taking a swim, enjoy historic **Wakulla Springs Lodge.** This Spanish-style inn, built in the 1930s of Tennessee marble, has unusual wood ceiling beams decorated with Florida scenes and flowers. The lodge dining room serves up Southern cooking at a reasonable cost. Wakulla Springs is 15 miles south of Tallahassee on Route 61. The lodge is open twenty-four hours; the park closes at dusk. Edward Ball Wakulla Springs State Park and Lodge, Wakulla Springs, FL 32305; (904) 224–5950. The park number is (904) 922–3633.

Civil War buffs will not want to miss the **Natural Bridge Battlefield State Historic Site.** Young cadets from West Florida Seminary (now Florida State University) and old men (Gadsden County Grays) joined Confederate forces to inflict heavy casualties on Union soldiers here on March 6, 1865. Thanks to their efforts, Tallahassee was the only southern capital east of the Mississippi that did not fall into Union hands. Each year, in early March, the battle is reenacted.

This is a fine place to do a little fishing in the St. Marks River or to have a picnic, but don't go looking for an impressive arch like Virginia's Natural Bridge. This was originally a place where the river flowed underground for a ways, but the county has modified the "bridge" for drainage purposes. The battlefield site is 10 miles southeast of Tallahassee. Take U.S. 363 to Woodville, then go east on Natural Bridge Road; (904) 925–6216. Free.

CENTRAL FLORIDA

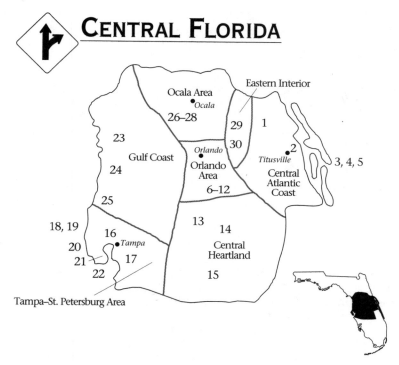

Ocala Area
•Ocala
26–28

Eastern Interior

29 1

30

23

Gulf Coast

24

Orlando
•
Orlando
Area
6–12

2
Titusville

3, 4, 5

Central
Atlantic
Coast

25

13

14
Central
Heartland

18, 19

16
•Tampa

20

21

17

15

22

Tampa–St. Petersburg Area

1. Daytona International Speedway
2. Great Outdoors RV/Nature & Golf Resort
3. Kennedy Space Center
4. Canaveral National Seashore
5. Merritt Island National Wildlife Refuge
6. Scenic Boat Tour
7. Loch Haven Park
8. Walt Disney World's Fort Wilderness Campground
9. Church Street Station
10. Gatorland
11. Medieval Times Dinner Tournament
12. Kissimmee Chain-of-Lakes
13. Bok Tower Gardens
14. Lake Kissimmee State Park
15. Highlands Hammock State Park
16. Safety Harbor Resort and Spa
17. Ybor Square
18. Honeymoon Island State Recreation Area
19. Caladesi Island
20. Suncoast Seabird Sanctuary
21. Salvador Dali Museum
22. Fort DeSoto Park
23. Homosassa Springs Wildlife Park
24. Weeki Wachee Springs
25. Tarpon Springs
26. Thoroughbred farms
27. Ocala National Forest
28. Silver Springs
29. Blue Springs State Park
30. Hontoon Island State Park

CENTRAL FLORIDA

CENTRAL ATLANTIC COAST

Ormond Beach and Daytona Beach owe their starts to the irrepressible Henry Flagler, who extended his railroad south and built the ornate Hotel Ormond in the late 1880s. The monied set was not far behind. When the Vanderbilts, Astors, and Goulds started wintering in Ormond Beach, it became known as the "millionaires' colony."

Rich men shipped their automobiles to Florida because the 500-foot-wide beach with its hard-packed sand was perfect for running flat out. By the turn of the century, Henry Ford, Louis Chevrolet, and R. E. Olds were comparing times on the beach's measured mile. Things moved quickly. In 1903 Alexander Winton set a world record of 68 mph on the sands of Daytona. A Stanley Steamer was clocked at 127.66 mph in 1906. The next year Ralph Owens made the first car trip from New York to Daytona in an amazing seventeen days. Thirteen auto speed records were set here between 1902 and 1935, earning the area the reputation as the "birthplace of speed."

Faster cars and larger crowds gradually outgrew the oval raceway that had been dug into the Daytona dunes. A 2½-mile asphalt track, opened in 1959, offered new challenges to the growing sport. World attention is riveted on the famous ✛ **Daytona International Speedway** during the July 4th 400-mile stock car race and its Daytona 500 in February. No tours of the Speedway are offered during races and special tests, but at other times a half-hour bus tour will fill you in on all the details. Open 9:00 A.M.–5:00 P.M. daily. The Speedway is at 1801 Speedway Boulevard. For tickets to special events, write Daytona International Speedway, 1801 International Speedway, Daytona, FL 32118; (904) 253–6711.

Daytona Beach's **Museum of Arts and Sciences** has a fine collection of Cuban paintings, a skeleton of a giant ground sloth, interesting fossils, and a planetarium. Open Tuesday through Friday 9:00 A.M.–4:00 P.M. and Saturday and Sunday noon–5:00 P.M. At 1040 Museum Boulevard in Tuscawilla Park; (904) 255–0285.

You don't have to be an RVer to stay at the ✛ **Great Outdoors RV/Nature & Golf Resort,** but most are. If you love the natural beauty of the outdoor world and enjoy golf, fishing, and the camaraderie of other like-minded folks, this is definitely the place for you.

No wonder this is considered one of the finest RV destinations in the South. Miles of scenic nature trails through forests and around lakes and wetlands reveal the beauty of these 3,000 acres. Woodlands shelter Sabal palms, holly, pines, wax myrtles, palmettos, and huge live oaks dripping with Spanish moss.

Walk quietly and keep an eagle eye out. You just might spot a pair of bald eagles, hawks, herons, anhingas, egrets, quail, wild turkeys, ducks, geese, raccoons, alligators, wild boar, bobcats, armadillos, and deer. About that bald eagle—it lives at the Great Outdoors in the only documented eagle's nest on a power line in the world and is protected by 1,000-foot development buffers.

Those who prefer their wildlife on the end of a hook will have lots of fishing stories to tell. This private fishing reserve includes twenty lakes and ponds (the largest, Lake Clifton, is 110 acres), each stocked to provide a natural balance of species and outstanding sportfishing. Largemouth bass, crappies, shellcrackers, bluegills, sunshine bass, and channel catfish lurk in these pristine waters.

During the season (November through March) "Fish-A-Thon" tournaments are held, each followed by an evening fish fry and awards ceremony. (They'll even bait your hooks and unhook the fish for you!) Wildlife Manager Jim Conley guides fishing trips both on and off the property and holds regular seminars on how to catch the "Big Ones."

The resort's centerpiece is an 18-hole, par-71, 6,542-yard championship golf course as handsome as it is challenging. Each hole was carefully designed to preserve the natural lay of the land with ponds, wooden bridges, white sand bunkers, and flowering foliage to enhance the scene. A full-time PGA pro oversees the clubhouse pro shop, teaching staff, driving range, and putting green. Yes, you may rent clubs and/or carts.

Besides fishing and golf, the Great Outdoors has two swimming pools (one heated and one screened), lighted tennis and shuffleboard courts, a health club with a well-equipped exercise room, sauna and steam rooms, a recreation hall with dance floor, a restaurant, a lounge, bathhouses with laundry facilities, a beauty salon, a hobby shop, a regulation croquet lawn, a library, a fire station, and a country store complete with deli.

A full schedule of activities ranges from nature programs featuring live animal shows and guest speakers, presentations by NASA space scientists on biomedical research, and the inside story of the space shuttle to Bible study groups.

A concierge in the Welcome Center lobby will help you (without charge) secure tee times, review local restaurant menus, and make dinner reservations or arrange for tickets to nearby attractions. The resort is less than an hour's drive from Orlando, the Disney attractions, Sea World, and Universal Studios; fewer than fifteen minutes from Kennedy Space Center and Spaceport USA; and a few minutes from blissfully uncrowded Atlantic beaches.

Landscaped RV sites include a paved driveway, a concrete pad and patio area, as well as full-service hookups for water, sewer, electricity, and cable TV. Telephone service is available. Florida Villas, Park Homes, and Resort Homes featuring RV parking right on the site are available for rent or sale. Owners may place their sites or homes in a rental pool providing a source of income while away.

There is no minimum stay for guests, but the minimum length for RVs is 18 feet. You can park overnight, enjoy a round of golf, and drive on, or you can move in and stay the rest of your life. Round-the-clock security includes a manned guard gate that controls access to the Great Outdoors for registered guests and owners.

This unique resort was the brainstorm of drugstore entrepreneur Jack Eckerd, a Floridian who has long been dedicated to environmental conservation. Mr. Eckerd thought it was high time someone designed an upscale RV park. Snow birds—those seeking a sunny getaway from northern winters—apparently appreciate all the amenities for they flock to the Great Outdoors in ever-increasing numbers.

The Great Outdoors Resort, 135 Plantation Drive, Titusville, FL 32780 is on Highway 50 just west of I–95, 6½ miles from Kennedy Space Center. (800) 621–2267 or (407) 269–5004.

The ◆ **Kennedy Space Center,** just south of Titusville, will test the limits of your imagination. At **Spaceport USA,** the visitor center at Kennedy Space Center, the past, present, and future of our country's inspiring probe into the mysteries of outer space are packed into one memorable visitor attraction. Admission and parking are free, as well as access to all indoor and outdoor space exhibits including *Satellites and You,* a forty-five-minute journey through a simulated future space station, the **Gallery of Spaceflight, NASA Art Exhibit,** the outdoor **Rocket Garden,** and live shows on a variety of current space-related topics presented in **Spaceport Theater.** A **Spaceman,** who loves to pose for photographs, appears for several hours daily.

You'll want to purchase tickets for a two-hour bus tour of Kennedy Space Center's **Launch Complex 39.** Highlights include camera stops near the Vehicle Assembly Building (one of the world's largest buildings), Space Shuttle launch pads A and B, and an authentic Saturn V Moon Rocket. Also available are tours of the historic **Cape Canaveral Air Force Station,** where the U.S. space program began in the early 1960s.

Don't miss the two impressive IMAX movies shown on a 5½-story screen in **IMAX Theater.** *The Dream is Alive* (thirty-seven minutes) shows NASA astronauts working and living in space. *Blue Planet* (forty-two minutes) takes an environmental look at our fragile planet from a 200-mile-high vantage point. The **Astronauts Memorial,** honoring the sixteen U.S. astronauts who gave their lives in the name of space exploration, was dedicated on May 9, 1991. This **Space Mirror Memorial,** which has the astronauts' names brilliantly lit by reflected sunlight, sits beside a quiet lagoon on six acres of land.

Spaceport USA is open from 9:00 A.M. to dusk every day except Christmas. Plan to arrive early. A typical visit lasts from five to six hours. Lunch is available at either the Orbit Cafeteria or the Lunch Pad restaurant. Spaceport USA is less busy on weekends than weekdays. Located on Florida's Space Coast one hour east of Orlando, Spaceport USA is off SR 405, NASA Parkway, 7 miles east of U.S. 1. Use exit 78 off I-95. Take SR 407 north if you're eastbound on the Beeline (SR 528). For Spaceport USA visitor or launch information, call the administrative office (open twenty-four hours daily) at (407) 452-2121 or write Spaceport USA, TWRS, Kennedy Space Center, FL 32899. For Space Coast visitor information call (407) 633-2110 or (800) USA-1969.

The Kennedy Space Center is flanked by the ◆ **Canaveral National Seashore** and the sprawling Merritt Island National Wildlife Refuge. All that's left of 600 years of fresh oyster dinners consumed by early Florida Indians is the 40-foot historic **Turtle Mound** at the northern tip of the National Seashore. Because this shell mound was the highest point of land for miles around, it served as an important landmark and appeared on sixteenth-century maps. Climb the boardwalk to the top for an impressive view of river and ocean. Turtle Mound is 10 miles south of New Smyrna Beach on SR A1A. Canaveral National Seashore is 7 miles east of Titusville. Open during daylight hours, the Turtle Mound is free.

Swimmers, surfers, and beachcombers head for Playalinda Beach at the south end of Canaveral where sea oats and shifting dunes create a lovely seascape. The National Seashore is one of the last sections of undeveloped beach on the east coast of Florida. The beach, open during daylight hours (except when the road is closed due to NASA launch-related activities), is free. Call (904) 428–3384 for information.

The ◆ **Merritt Island National Wildlife Refuge** protects more endangered species of birds, mammals, and reptiles than any other area of the continental United States. The Audubon Society has registered one of the highest counts of bird species in the country here. Gulls, terns, egrets, herons, ibis, and storks are a common sight. You may even be lucky enough to spot the pretty pink roseate spoonbill or the endangered bald eagle. Open during daylight hours; (407) 861–0667. Free.

If you are intrigued by tropical foliage, you will want to see the **Botanical Garden** on the grounds of the Florida Institute of Technology in Melbourne with more than 300 species of palms, ferns, and other plants. The institute is on Country Club Road, a mile south of New Haven Avenue, Melbourne; (407) 984–2974.

ORLANDO AREA

The **Maitland Art Center** is a special place. Originally designed to be a retreat for avant garde artists, it is now an attractive complex housing a fascinating permanent collection and monthly rotating exhibits by contemporary artists. The buildings, adorned with murals and ornamental carvings in Aztec-Mayan motif, are well worth seeing as is the tranquil garden and courtyard area. When you visit the Garden Chapel with its trellised walkway, you'll understand why this is such a popular place for weddings. Maitland Art Center, 231 W. Packwood Avenue, Maitland, FL 32751. Open 10:00 A.M.–4:30 P.M. Monday through

Friday and noon–4:30 P.M. on Saturday and Sunday. Call (407) 539–2181. Free.

If you love birds you'll be very happy at the **Audubon House,** which includes a gallery, a large collection of live birds in an aviary, and a gift shop featuring books on birds and recordings of bird calls. Its **Center for Birds of Prey** is one of the leading raptor rehabilitation centers in the state. You are encouraged to report injured or orphaned birds of prey to (407) 645–3826. Audubon House is at 1101 Audubon Way, Maitland, FL 32751. Open Tuesday through Saturday 10:00 A.M.–4:00 P.M. The aviary is closed on Sunday. The Audubon House phone number is (407) 644–0190.

The largest collection of Tiffany glass and jewelry in the world resides at the **Morse Museum of American Art** in Winter Park. This gallery features late-nineteenth- and twentieth-century art and decorative arts including leaded stained glass windows, lamps, blown glass, pottery, paintings, and furniture. Open Tuesday through Saturday 9:30 A.M.–4:00 P.M. and Sunday 1:00–4:00 P.M. The Morse Gallery of Art, 445 Park Avenue North, Winter Park, FL 32789; (407) 645–5311.

Winter Park's **Rollins College** has a beautiful campus with even more going for it than the attractive Spanish/Mediterranean architecture. The college's **Cornell Fine Arts Museum** with three galleries of rotating art exhibits is open to the public year-round 10:00 A.M.–5:00 P.M. Tuesday through Friday and 1:00–5:00 P.M. Saturday and Sunday; (407) 646–2526.

One fun way to really appreciate this lovely lake-dotted area is to take a ◆**Scenic Boat Tour**. The boat leaves daily between 10:00 A.M. and 4:00 P.M. from the eastern foot of Morse Boulevard on Lake Osceola in Winter Park. The one-hour narrated ride takes you through various Winter Park lakes and canals, by estates, the Isle of Sicily, Kraft Azalea Gardens, and Rollins College. Scenic Boat Tour, 312 E. Morse Blvd., Lake Osceola, Winter Park, FL 32789; (407) 644–4056.

Central Florida's major city, Orlando, was settled by soldiers who decided to stick around after the Seminole wars in the 1830s. It was little more than a cattle country trading post until the railroad's arrival brought an influx of people and business in 1880. Then the town eased into a string of unremarkable years as a shipping center for citrus fruits and vegetables.

47

Over the years Orlando capitalized on its best features—fifty-four lakes within the city limits and a year-round average temperature of 72 degrees. The community protected its venerable groves of live oaks by creating forty-seven parks. A loyal contingent of northerners who appreciated both the beauty and the climate enjoyed the town's relaxed pace each winter.

Those were the days before the nation's launch into space from nearby Cape Canaveral and before the coming of Walt Disney World. The city is still pretty with all its lakes and parks intact, but the relaxed pace is a memory. Orlando is one of the fastest growing metropolitan areas in the United States, and the face of central Florida has been forever changed.

◆ **Loch Haven Park** in Orlando offers a cluster of quality attractions. Parking is easy and you may spend all day enjoying the **Orlando Museum of Art,** Orange County Historical Museum, and Orlando Science Center. The Art Center has a growing permanent collection of twentieth-century American art, pre-Columbian artifacts, African art, and changing exhibitions from internationally renowned museums and private collections. Gallery hours are 9:00 A.M.–5:00 P.M. Tuesday through Saturday and noon–5:00 P.M. Sunday; (407) 896–4231. Free.

The **Orange County Historical Museum** began in 1942 when a group of women set up a pioneer kitchen in the 1892 red-brick courthouse for a county-wide centennial. It has evolved into a handsome museum that will take you on a trip down memory lane. Here you'll travel back to the time when Florida was a wilderness, learn about the Big Freeze of 1894–95 that destroyed the citrus industry, and ride the roller coaster real estate boom-and-bust days of the 1920s. On display are a 1,000-year-old Timucuan Indian canoe, a newspaper composing room in the hot-type tradition, a Victorian parlor, and the hide of a 15-foot alligator. Open Monday through Saturday 9:00 A.M.–5:00 P.M. and Sunday noon–5:00 P.M. Orange County Historical Museum, Loch Haven Park, 812 East Rollins Street, Orlando, FL 32803; (407) 897–6350.

Out the back door you'll find Fire Station No. 3, **Orlando's oldest standing firehouse,** which operates as an extension of the Historical Museum. This captures the flavor of the early bucket brigade days and comes complete with a traditional sliding pole, an 1885 hose cart, and even a potbellied stove. It's open Monday through Saturday 9:00 A.M.–5:00 P.M. and Sunday noon–5:00 P.M.; (407) 897–6350.

Those who find their earth weight discouraging may take consolation in learning their moon weight, one of many neat things you can do at the **Orlando Science Center.** This is one of those places where you learn a great deal while having a good time, and it is especially good for families. Ask about the daily planetarium shows. Open Monday through Thursday 9:00 A.M.–5:00 P.M., Friday 9:00 A.M.–9:00 P.M., Saturday 9:00 A.M.–5:00 P.M., and Sunday noon–5:00 P.M. Orlando Science Center and John Young Planetarium, Loch Haven Park, 810 E. Rollins Street, Orlando, FL 32803; (407) 896–7151.

When the hustle and bustle of Orlando is too much for you, a walk through **Leu Gardens** provides a welcome tonic. More than fifty acres of trees, flowering shrubs, roses, camellias, orchids, and azaleas border Lake Rowena. Several floral varieties bloom most of the year, but the big show is from December to March as this is primarily a winter garden. A museum house, which shows how a well-to-do Florida family lived at the turn-of-the-century, is open Tuesday through Saturday 10:00 A.M.–3:30 P.M. and Sunday and Monday 1:00–3:00 P.M. Tours are on the half hour. The garden is open 9:00 A.M.–5:00 P.M. daily except for Christmas. Leu House and Gardens, 1920 N. Forest Avenue, Orlando, FL 32803; (407) 246–2620.

Camping sounds like fun, but you want a real vacation complete with daily maid service, cable TV, and air-conditioning. Surprise! You can have it all at ◆**Walt Disney World's Fort Wilderness Campground.** More than 400 Fleetwood trailers are fully equipped with dishes and cooking utensils and dishwashers. Most sleep six. While enjoying all the comforts and conveniences of a fine hotel, you can also have the rustic beauty of the great outdoors.

Hearty fare and wholesome fun is close by. The *Hoop-Dee-Doo-Revue* at Pioneer Hall is the second-longest-running show at Walt Disney World. A cast of six "stagecoach passengers" keeps everyone in stitches for almost two hours. In between laughs fill up on fried chicken, barbecued ribs, corn on the cob, and strawberry shortcake. Afterward, it's home-sweet-home to your trailer under the trees. For information about Fort Wilderness, write Walt Disney World Central Reservations, P.O. Box 10100, Lake

Buena Vista, FL 32830, or call (407) 934–7639.

Just in case you're in the mood for an early morning hot air balloon ride over Orlando, Church Street Station is standing by. Start the day with coffee and orange juice and polish off your aerial adventure with a champagne brunch at **Lili Marlene's Restaurant.** A day to store in the memory forever! Call (407) 841–8787.

◆**Church Street Station** also features Phineas Phogg's Balloon Works (purveyors of balloons, burgers, and boogie), Apple Annie's Courtyard, and Cheyenne Saloon and Opera House. Nickel beer night is Wednesday, and western and Indian antiques are available at Buffalo Trading Co. It's impossible to take advantage of all the excitement at Church Street Station, but you might as well try. This complete dining, shopping, and entertainment complex is open every day 11:00 A.M.–2:00 A.M. and features twenty live shows nightly. Church Street Station is at 129 W. Church Street, Orlando, FL 32801; (407) 422–2434.

While you're in the neighborhood, ◆**Gatorland** (next door to Tupperware) should be in your plans. Don't worry about the huge alligator jaws you walk through to enter. This isn't just another hokey attraction, but a fine zoo with more than 5,000 alligators and crocodiles (Gatorland claims to be the world's largest alligator farm attraction) and some rather exotic animals including snakes, birds, and monkeys. An interesting artificial insemination program for alligators is in full swing here.

Allow plenty of time to stroll the boardwalk through the eerie beauty of a cypress swamp. This sanctuary, lush with wild orchids and ferns, offers a welcome reprieve from the hectic pace some sightseers set for themselves. Open daily 8:00 A.M.–8:00 P.M. (8:00 A.M.–6:00 P.M. during the winter), Gatorland is on U.S. 441 next to Tupperware. Mailing address: 14501 S. Orange Blossom Trail, Orlando, FL 32837. (407) 855–5496.

A novel way to see the "real" Florida is by piloting your own airboat. Explore **wild cypress swamps,** where tall waterbirds stalk their supper and trees are festooned with Spanish moss. You'll get the hang of the steering bar right away. Just pull back if you want to go right and push forward to go left. Only ten minutes from Walt Disney World, this lovely natural spot can also be seen by electric boat and/or canoe. Boats and canoes can be rented at **Airboat Rentals U-Drive,** which is 6 miles east of I–4 on U.S. 192 in Kissimmee; (407) 847–3672.

Aaah, the romance of medieval times when brave knights defended their kingdoms and castles were scenes of great feasts and much revelry. This is now a possible dream thanks to ◆ **Medieval Times Dinner and Tournament.** Slip back to Europe in the eleventh century and admire valiant knights on richly attired horses. A "serving wench" brings a delicious four-course dinner, which you eat with your hands. (Remember, this is the year of grace 1092.)

Spectacular pageantry, splendid horses galloping at full tilt, and knights who duel to the death (well, almost) combine to make quite an evening. Just when you thought chivalry was dead, a knight shows up and throws you a flower. A knight to remember! Medieval Times is on U.S. 192 in Kissimmee. Medieval Times, P.O. Box 422385, Kissimmee, FL 34742 (800–229–8300) The number for the castle in Kissimmee is (407) 396–1518.

Kissimmee had a long proud heritage as the capital of cattle country before being billed as the Gateway to Walt Disney World. Spanish explorers brought livestock to the New World, and when Florida became a United States territory in 1821, the open range and scrub cattle descended from Spanish cows lured homesteaders to the Florida frontier. South of Orlando's dazzle, hundreds of cattle ranches and a thriving beef and dairy industry prosper. The cowboy's own brand of excitement rears up twice a year at Florida's largest and oldest professional rodeo, **Kissimmee's Silver Spurs.** For information about these special events or about attending a weekly cattle auction (Wednesdays) contact the Kissimmee–St. Cloud Convention and Visitors Bureau, P.O. Box 422007, Kissimmee, FL 34742–2007; (407) 847–5000.

In Kissimmee don't forget to visit the **Monument of States,** made of stones from every state in the Union. The 70-foot structure was built by Kissimmee citizens in 1943 with 1,500 stones from every state and twenty-one foreign countries. Near the lakefront in downtown Kissimmee.

Kissimmee lies at the head of the 50-mile-long ◆ **Kissimmee Chain-of-Lakes,** and those who want to experience central Florida at its natural best should see it from the water. Far from the madding crowd are quiet lagoons and blue herons picking their way through water hyacinths. Besides being splendidly scenic, this is one of the country's best bass fishing grounds. The sunset is in living color, the view is multidimensional, and the big sound is a night chorus of tree frogs and cicadas. Houseboats and assorted other craft may be rented on Lake Tohopekaliga. Take U.S. 192 to SR 17-92 south, then at the second or third traffic light, turn left to lakefront. For information call Parks and Recreation; (407) 847–2388.

Originally founded in 1972 as a research center for the production and distribution of snake venoms, **Reptile World Serpentarium** now offers close-up views of poisonous snakes being milked. Time your visit to be on hand during one of three daily venom programs given at 11:00 A.M., 2:00 P.M., and 5:00 P.M. You'll see turtles and alligators as well as cobras, mambas, vipers, rattlesnakes, and giant pythons. The gift shop has an excellent selection of books on reptiles. Open Tuesday through Sunday 9:00 A.M.–5:30 P.M. Closed the month of September. Located 4 miles east of St. Cloud on U.S. 192. Reptile World Serpentarium, 5705 E. Bronson Memorial Highway, St. Cloud, FL 32769; (407) 892–6905.

CENTRAL HEARTLAND

The central heartland of Florida seems, from certain viewpoints, like a huge sprawling sea of orange trees. Tidy parallel rows of trees undulate off into the distance like dark green waves. In the midst of citrus country are modern packing plants and frozen juice processors well equipped to handle the huge harvest. Many highway fruit and juice stands cater to tourists intent on carrying some fresh Florida fruit home to their winter-bound northern friends. At **Orange Ring** you can sample a free glass of orange juice and purchase any number of goodies including orange butter and chocolate alligators. The packing plant, behind the gift shop, gives brief tours during the week. Orange Ring, P.O. Drawer 2107, Haines City, FL 33845; (813) 422–1938. On U.S. 27 north of Haines City.

Watch citrus candy being made in copper kettles at **Davidson of Dundee Citrus Candy Factory** on U.S. 27 in Dundee. Open daily 8:00 A.M.–6:00 P.M., but candy is not made on weekends. Davidson of Dundee, P.O. Box 800, Dundee, FL 33838; (813) 439–1698.

Cypress Gardens in Winter Haven has been a popular tourist destination for many years. The Pope family began extensive landscaping on the shores of Lake Eloise in the 1930s. In 1942 they enlivened the botanical beauty by adding ski shows. Amateur and professional photographers as well as moviemakers are drawn to the gorgeous scenery, and spectators cheer the talented skiers' mastery of the newest tricks.

Today Cypress Gardens features, along with magnificent gardens and thrilling waterski shows, a variety of attractions including "Cypress Roots," a walk down memory lane complete with a display of cameras from the twenties to the seventies; Cypress Junction, an elaborate model railroad; a Russian ice-skating show; and "When Radios Were Radios," commemorating the nostalgic years of radio. Kids love the rides in "Carousel Cove" and the old-fashioned circus daredevil acts. Do not—repeat, *do not*—leave without experiencing Cypress Gardens' **Wings of Wonder,** a butterfly conservatory where visitors encounter more than fifty colorful species of butterflies from around the world. Cypress Gardens is open year-round 9:30 A.M.–5:30 P.M. The gardens are off U.S. 27, 22 miles south of I–4 between Orlando and Tampa. Cypress Gardens, P.O. Box 1, Cypress Gardens, FL 33884; (813) 324–2111.

Chalet Suzanne Country Inn and Restaurant, in Lake Wales, opens itself up like the petals of a flower. First you discover a tiny whimsical pastel village with its thirty rooms each decorated in different combinations of Swedish tile, Spanish ironwork, and Moorish mosaics. Then sample some of the Chalet's famous romaine soup in the intimate Old World dining room. (No wonder this soup was chosen to go to the moon with the crew of Apollo 15.) Each place is set with fine china, perhaps German porcelain or elegant Limoges, and your view overlooks a private lake.

Then you come upon the Chapel where you can buy all manner of fine glassware and antiques, the Wine Dungeon, the Wreck Room, the Soup Cannery, and a ceramic salon where Lilliana and Boz Birvis are turning out treasures. Chalet Suzanne is one surprise after another, and that, and the good taste with which everything is done, accounts for its success as well as its charm.

Gourmet Magazine labeled Chalet Suzanne food "glorious" and surely it is, but be warned that the prices are also glorious. If a glance at the lunch menu withers your wallet, ask for the soup and sandwich du jour (unlisted). That way you can treat yourself to a fine meal without taking out a new mortgage. Owned and operated by the Hinshaw family since 1931, Chalet Suzanne is between Cypress Gardens and Bok Tower Gardens just off U.S. 27 and 17A. Or come by plane and land on the 2,450-foot private airstrip! Chalet Suzanne, 3800 Chalet Drive, Lake Wales, FL 33853; (813) 676–6011. Expensive.

The 128-acre ◆**Bok Tower Gardens** in Lake Wales have been devoted to peace and beauty since 1928. Listed in the National Register of Historic Places, the gardens and tower were dedicated to the American people because Edward Bok, a Dutch immigrant, wanted to make America "a bit more beautiful" because he had lived here. The hushed atmosphere of the surroundings is interrupted only by a daily bell serenade (3:00 P.M.) from the 205-foot "singing" tower, which has been called one of the world's great carillons. Enjoy the azaleas, camellias, magnolias, and many birds. Surrounded by citrus orchards, this is the place to come in the spring when the air is heavy with the scent of orange blossoms. The gardens are open every day 8:00 A.M.–5:00 P.M. Located 3 miles north of Lake Wales off CR 17A (Burns Avenue). Bok Tower Gardens, Lake Wales, FL 33859-3810; (813) 676–1408.

◆**Lake Kissimmee State Park** is way off the beaten path, but worth it. The park consists of more than 5,000 acres bordered by lakes Kissimmee, Tiger, and Rosalie. The lakes, floodplain prairies, marshes, and pine flatwoods are home to a variety of wildlife, including the rare Florida panther. (Don't count on seeing a panther; they're very shy.) This is a fine spot to boat, hike, picnic, and camp. For an excellent view of Lake Kissimmee, try the top of the observation platform.

One of the best features of the park is a reconstructed **1876 Cow Camp** with scrub cows and "cow hunters." (They will quickly tell you they do not care to be called cowboys.) Here you can learn firsthand about the bustling cattle business on the south Florida frontier and see one of the few remaining herds of scrub cows in existence.

As you walk down the trail to the camp, you travel back to the year 1876. The cow hunter may be having a cup of coffee near his campfire, or perhaps is rounding up cows for the long cattle drive to the west coast of Florida. The cattlemen were paid in gold Spanish doubloons. The cow hunter welcomes your questions, but don't bother asking about anything that happened

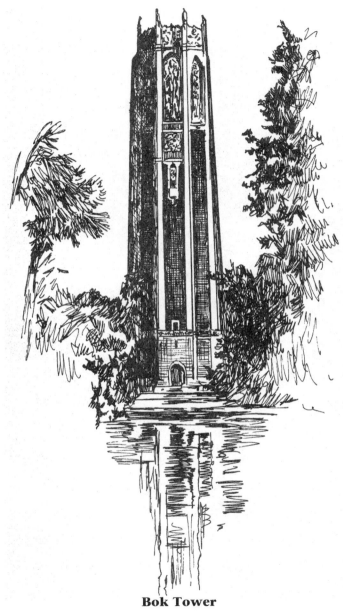

Bok Tower

after 1876. He will just look very puzzled and won't know what you're talking about.

The cow camp is only open on weekends and holidays 9:30 A.M.–4:30 P.M. The park is open daily 7:00 A.M. to sunset year-round. Lake Kissimmee State Park, 14248 Camp Mack Road, Lake Wales, FL 33853. The park is 15 miles east of Lake Wales, off Camp Mack Road. Call (813) 696–1112.

Follow nature trails and boardwalks through the jungles, cypress swamps, and tropical wilderness of ◆ **Highlands Hammock State Park.** Your stroll will be rewarded with glimpses of sunning alligators and rare orchids. You'll also want to visit the C.C.C. museum and ride the park's "trackless train" on regularly scheduled wildlife tours. A good place to bike (rentals available), picnic, and camp. Highlands Hammock is open daily 8:00 A.M. until sunset. Located 6 miles west of Sebring, off U.S. 27-634; (813) 386–6094.

Florida Southern College, in Lakeland, boasts the world's largest concentration of architecture by Frank Lloyd Wright. Wright's design for these seven unconventional buildings called for steel for strength, sand for Florida, and glass to bring the outdoors in. The steeple of the **Annie Pfeiffer Chapel,** designed as a chime resonator, casts shifting shadows into the interior. Tinted glass squares filter colored light in during the day. The low esplanade, a sheltered walkway, was obviously not designed with today's basketball players in mind; no ceiling or doorway is much over 6 feet tall! The Science Building, more than 400 feet long with a planetarium at the southern end, is the largest structure, and some say the most magnificent.

The lakeside campus is open to the public 8:00 A.M.–5:00 P.M. weekdays. Pick up a map for a self-guided tour in the Administration Building. Florida Southern College, Lakeland, FL 33801-5698; (813) 680–4111. From Orlando, go west on I–4 to the U.S. 98 south exit 18. Turn right on U.S. 98 to Memorial Boulevard. Go left on Memorial Boulevard to Ingraham Avenue. Turn right and stay on Ingraham until you reach the campus. Free.

TAMPA–ST. PETERSBURG AREA

Spanish explorers discovered Tampa in the sixteenth century. They also discovered the resident Indians who resisted being converted to Catholicism and resented the European urge for conquering. The resulting clash of interests led to bloodshed frequently over the years.

One of those early Spanish explorers, Hernando DeSoto, discovered the mineral springs of Safety Harbor, which he named the "Springs of the Holy Spirit," on May 18, 1539. He was not the first to be attracted by the springs. Various Indian tribes, inhabiting the area as long as 12,000 years ago, believed the springs had curative powers.

During a fight with the Seminoles, Colonel William J. Bailey captured a sick Indian who volunteered to be a guide if the Colonel would take him to the healing springs. The Colonel bought the springs and surrounding land from the government in the 1850s, the first person to own the springs after the United States acquired Florida from the Spanish.

In the early 1900s, five different springs were identified that "cured" a variety of ailments from dropsy to psoriasis. Before long northerners were visiting the spa to "take the waters." In 1964 Safety Harbor Resort was officially listed as a historical landmark by the U.S. Department of the Interior.

All well and good but what's going on at the springs today? The answer is plenty, and, in keeping with tradition, it's all very healthy and restorative to both body and spirit. The ❖ **Safety Harbor Resort and Spa** offers more than fifty rejuvenating, relaxing, and pampering spa and salon services ranging from deep tissue sports massages, facials, loofah salt glows, and herbal wraps to aromatherapy.

Lifestyle and fitness classes, tennis clinics, and golf on nearby courses are also featured. Guests may attend a lecture on healthy feet, "Supermarket Savvy" (an educational trip to a nearby grocery store), or a myriad of other offerings designed to enhance their well-being.

One of America's oldest spa resorts, Safety Harbor is Florida's only spa resort featuring natural mineral springs. On arrival, guests find a bottle of specially filtered mineral water in their rooms from the springs beneath the hotel. The spa, consistently ranked as having one of the top aquatic programs in the country, offers everything from Water Walking and Water Aerobics to Water Butt Busters. After a workout guests may relax in a Turkish steam bath or a Finnish sauna.

The resort's spa menu offers nutritious, low-fat, low-calorie, gourmet cuisine. A full-fare menu is also offered with emphasis on naturally grown fresh Florida fruits and vegetables. Located on the shores of Old Tampa Bay, Safety Harbor Resort is about twenty minutes from two major international airports—Tampa International Airport and St. Petersburg/Clearwater International Airport—and is easily reached from I–75 and I–4. Call for directions. Safety Harbor Resort and Spa, 105 N. Bayshore Drive, P.O. Box 248, Safety Harbor, FL 34695-0248; (813) 726–1161 or (800) 237–0155.

Safety Harbor Museum of Regional History, a tiny gem of a museum featuring rare treasures of prehistoric Indians and other exhibits of local interest, is a short walk from the resort. Fascinating dioramas enlighten visitors to the rich history of this area as well as the evolution of the American Indian throughout the Southeast.

Located in Safety Harbor on Old Tampa Bay, the museum is on a historic Indian burial site. Open Tuesday through Saturday 10:00 A.M.–4:00 P.M. and Sunday 1:00–4:00 P.M. The Safety Harbor Museum of Regional History, 329 S. Bayshore Boulevard, Safety Harbor, FL 34695; (813) 726–1668.

Tampa's real development began in 1883 when Henry B. Plant linked Tampa with Jacksonville by a combination of railroad and steamship connections. Henry Plant, competing with East Coast railroad tycoon Henry Flagler, erected the ostentatious Moorish-style **Tampa Bay Hotel** in 1891. Sporting silver Turkish minarets, the palatial hotel ushered in Tampa's era as a fashionable winter resort for well-heeled northerners. Costing a cool $3.5 million, it was regarded in its day as the most elegant and most expensive hotel in the world.

Today it is considered the finest example of Moorish architecture in the Western Hemisphere and is home to the **University of Tampa.** To see some of the furniture and art of the late Victorian era, visit the **Henry B. Plant Museum** in a wing of the main university building. Open Tuesday through Saturday 10:00 A.M.–4:00 P.M. and Sunday noon–4:00 P.M. The museum/university is at 401 W. Kennedy Boulevard at the Hillsborough River; (813) 254–1891.

Today Tampa is a major industrial metropolis and busy shipping center for a great variety of products including phosphates, citrus fruits, and cattle. At day's end you may be interested in watching shrimp boats unload their catch at the **shrimp docks** on the Twenty-second Street Causeway. Free.

Citizens have worked hard to preserve Tampa's heritage. The Hispanic community centered in **Ybor City** has been largely returned to its late-nineteenth-century appearance. Cigar makers demonstrate the art of hand rolling in restored ✦**Ybor Square,** a complex of shops and restaurants. Ybor City, which is a National Historic District, is bounded by Columbus Drive, Fifth Avenue, Nebraska Avenue, and Twenty-second Street.

Around the turn of the century, the Ferlita Bakery flourished along with Ybor City and the cigar industry. In the "Cigar Capital of the World" workers lived very well indeed, and a boom-town atmosphere prevailed. The bakery (listed on the National Register of Historic Sites) has now been transformed by the state of Florida into a museum where you can learn about Tampa's Latin community and see old photos, cigar industry artifacts, and the original 1896 bakery oven. The **Ybor City State Museum,** 1818 Ninth Avenue, Tampa, FL 33605. Open 9:00 A.M.–5:00 P.M. Tuesday through Saturday. (813) 247–6323.

Tampa's distinct Latin flavor is retained in its Spanish shops, restaurants, and the general ambience of the community. You may see long loaves of Cuban bread rolled out by hand at **La Segunda Central Bakery** if you arrive before 9:00 A.M. Go around to the back door and watch as bakers shape the dough and place a single strand of palmetto leaf on each yard-long loaf. The bakery is at 2512 N. Fifteenth Street in Ybor City.

You may buy a fresh loaf from the store, or order a Cuban sandwich (looking for all the world like a sub) for lunch at a number of Spanish restaurants on E. Seventh Street in Ybor City. If you choose **La Tropicana,** you'll notice one table in the back that looks different from all the rest. It even has its own old-fashioned upright phone used to gather news for the local scandal sheet. If you have something to contribute, stop in at La Tropicana at 1822 E. Seventh Street. Those who don't go for subs might like the deviled crab or potato stuffed with meat.

There's always a possibility you'll get caught in a hurricane, but then that's all part of the fun (and learning) going on at MOSI, the **Museum of Science and Industry.** The museum has tripled in size to become the largest science center in the

Southeast with Florida's only IMAX Dome Theater. Take part in all kinds of fascinating experiments in this hands-on center, and be sure to see the butterfly encounter and the planetarium. Exhibits and demonstrations explain the major scientific phenomena and industries of Florida—energy, weather, electricity, water, flight and space, and the environment. Don't miss the "Amazing You," a tour of the human body from DNA cells to organs to individuals. Recently expanded with many new things to see and do, the museum is in North Tampa 3 miles east of I–275 and is open 9:00 A.M.–4:30 P.M. Sunday through Thursday and 9:00 A.M.–9:00 P.M. Friday. Museum of Science and Industry, 4801 E. Fowler Avenue, Tampa, FL 33617; (813) 987–6300.

Get out your skateboard. Put on your jogging shoes or your roller skates. Tampa boasts nothing less than the longest continuous sidewalk in the world. **Bayshore Boulevard**'s 6½-mile sidewalk is the focus of much activity as folks take advantage of this scenic stretch bordering one of the city's oldest and finest residential areas. During a hurricane this is where the water comes ashore, and daring surfers replace joggers and skaters. You don't have to be quite that adventurous, but this just might be a good time to find out what it feels like to walk half a dozen miles.

One of the interesting things you'll see along Bayshore Boulevard is the *Jose Gasparilla,* the world's only fully rigged pirate ship. The ship stars during the annual **Gasparilla Invasion** held each February when businessmen-turned-buccaneers take over. The ensuing month-long festivities include torchlight parades, marathons, and fancy dress balls. For information: Tampa/Hillsborough Convention and Visitors Association, 111 E. Madison Street, Tampa, FL 33602; (813) 223–1111.

You'll enjoy a "wild" safari on the **Serengeti Plain at Busch Gardens.** Four hundred head of exotic big game including giraffes, zebras, elephants, gazelles, and Cape buffalo roam at will as you cross the veldtlike plain via monorail, steam locomotive, or skyride. Much more than an amusement park, Busch Gardens, with its African motif and more than 3,000 animals, is regarded as one of the top four zoos in the country. Be sure to pay your respects to the rare white Bengal tigers and see Eagle Canyon, a newly constructed natural habitat display for American bald eagles and golden eagles located at the entrance to the

Anheuser-Busch Brewery; (800) 372–1797.

Bern's Steak House is as much an experience as it is a restaurant. The menu looks like an engineering spec sheet, the place is ornate (to put it mildly), and the emphasis is on doing things differently. Perhaps that explains why the gargantuan wine list is almost too heavy to lift. (To have your own copy, you'll have to part with more than $30. Don't try to walk off with one—it's chained to the table.)

From their own organic farm to the world's largest wine cellar, the emphasis at Bern's is on putting together the perfect meal. Waiters train a minimum of one year working in every station in the restaurant before being permitted in the dining room. Cress seeds from London are sprouted right in the kitchen and caviar is flown in daily. Your steak is cut, trimmed, and weighed only after you have placed your order. Coffee beans are hand-sorted and the whole operation is coordinated by computer.

All this information (and much more) is on your menu, but is it all true? Yes. Bern's encourages tours of the kitchen and wine cellar throughout the evening. Between courses, diners take advantage of this offer to inspect the immaculate facilities and cavernous (and cold—take a sweater) wine cellar. They even get to see the sprouts sprouting.

The final course of coffee and dessert is served in your own private room upstairs, which comes complete with a color TV that you control. This way you can watch the restaurant musicians (and request a favorite song on your own phone) or choose from other TV entertainment. You may dance if you wish or simply spend the rest of the evening trying to select the perfect drink from a list of 1,000 dessert wines. The choice of dessert is not so overwhelming. Besides, you can't go wrong ordering Triple Chocolate. Bern's Steak House, 1208 S. Howard Avenue, Tampa, FL 33606; (813) 251–2421. In Florida: (800) 282–1547. Expensive.

Take the scenic drive on Dunedin Beach Causeway to ✤ **Honeymoon Island State Recreation Area** and notice the large pines on the island's northern loop trail. This is one of a very few virgin slash pine stands in south Florida, as well as an important nesting site for the threatened osprey. A wide variety of plants and birds, including several endangered species, call this lovely island home. You may want to picnic, swim, fish, or catch the ferry to Caladesi Island. Honeymoon Island is at No. 1

Causeway Boulevard west of U.S. 19A; (813) 469–5942. ❖**Caladesi Island,** located off Dunedin, is one of Florida's few unspoiled barrier islands. Catch the ferry (which leaves hourly, weather permitting) from Dunedin Beach on Honeymoon Island and spend some time at this attractive state park. Accessible only by boat, this is a good place to swim, skin dive, boat, picnic, or beachcomb for shells. The park has almost 3 miles of sandy beach, a ridge of virgin pine flatwoods, and a mangrove swamp. A 60-foot observation tower offers views of the area and of vessels in the Gulf. The island is north of Dunedin off U.S. 19A. For information call the ferry (813) 734–1501 or the park (813) 469–5917.

Remember the old sugar cane mill, the railroad depot, and the bandstand in the middle of the park? Open-air **Heritage Park** has these and more. Travel back in time to the early days of Pinellas County while browsing the old barn, church, cottage, loghouse, and other structures. A guide in period dress will show you around, or you can poke about on your own. How did those early settlers manage? At least some of the answers are here in this pretty pine and palmetto park. Open Tuesday through Saturday 10:00 A.M.–4:00 P.M., Sunday 1:00–4:00 P.M. Closed Monday. Heritage Park, 11909 125th Street North, Largo, FL 34644; (813) 582–2123. Free.

The ❖**Suncoast Seabird Sanctuary** is dedicated to the rescue, repair, recuperation, and, hopefully, the release of rehabilitated wild birds. It all began when Ralph Heath nursed an injured cormorant back to health in 1971. Word spread and soon people were leaving injured birds on his doorstep. Today the sanctuary is home to more than 500 birds and as many as twenty injured birds are brought daily. Unfortunately more than 90 percent of these injuries are directly or indirectly related to human beings, who seem adept at throwing the delicate balance of nature out of kilter.

This nonprofit organization (supported entirely by donations) has a full-time staff of fifteen, a hospital complete with intensive-care room, and an annual budget of $700,000. So far nearly 35,000 birds have been returned to the wild.

A recent success story involved the release of a southern bald eagle. Some permanently injured birds become full-time residents. You may watch brown pelicans building nests with branches and rearing young in captivity. Notice the contingent of perfectly well birds perching on top of the aviary. Isn't it thoughtful of them to visit their hospitalized friends? Bring a camera and leave a donation or, better yet, fill out an application to adopt a bird. The sanctuary is open seven days a week 9:00 A.M. until dark. Suncoast Seabird Sanctuary, 18328 Gulf Boulevard, Indian Shores, FL 34635; (813) 391–6211. Free.

A couple of sea turtle hunters returning from the Gulf were the first to see **John's Pass** in Madeira Beach. (It didn't exist until the hurricane of 1848.) Juan Levique was the one who spotted the changed coastline, so naturally it came to be known as John's Pass. Today an early Florida fishing village atmosphere prevails. Boutiques and shops like **Holy Shirt** and the **Fudge and Cookie Factory** cater to tourists' whims. Choose from a large selection of beachwear, jewelry, stained glass, or hand-crafted items. This is a fine place to fish, charter a boat, or just walk the boardwalk with an eye out for playful dolphins.

An excellent way to start the day is at the **Friendly Fisherman Seafood Restaurant** with a Boardwalk Breakfast. You can't miss with a basket of hot corn fritters. Later in the day, you can stop in and munch on grouper cheeks (no bones!). The Friendly Fisherman is on the boardwalk at John's Pass in Madeira Beach. Inexpensive.

No wonder folks flock to St. Petersburg with its exquisite beaches and 361 days of sunshine each year. Settled in the 1840s, St. Petersburg came to life in 1885 when Peter Demens extended his Orange Belt Railroad into the peninsula and named the settlement for his Russian birthplace. Imagine a place so confident of its sunshine that one of its newspapers gives away all the street editions if the weather remains cloudy for the entire day.

The world's largest collection of art by Spanish surrealist Salvador Dali can be found in St. Petersburg. The $35 million collection features oil paintings, watercolors, drawings, graphics, and sculptures. The fascination here is to see Dali's development from 1914 to 1980. The ◆**Salvador Dali Museum** is open Tuesday through Saturday 9:30 A.M.–5:30 P.M. and Sunday noon–5:30 P.M. It is located in Poynter Park on the waterfront in south St. Petersburg at 1000 Third Street S., St. Petersburg, FL 33701; (813) 823–3767.

If you want a touch of history in your vacation itinerary, you will delight in the grand wedding cake of a hotel known as the **Don Ce Sar.** Take off your rose-colored glasses and it's still pink—really pink, as in flamingos, Easter eggs, and bubble gum.

Unfortunately a glorious opening night in January 1928 was followed by the stock market crash of 1929. Despite the patronage of such prominent guests as Scott and Zelda Fitzgerald, Clarence Darrow, and Babe Ruth, the dismal days of the 1930s took their toll. Tourism had all but disappeared when the army bought it during the war for a song and turned it into a hospital. (The Bistro served as the morgue.) Deterioration and neglect pointed toward the Don's demise until a Save the Don committee worked a near miracle and rescued it during the 1970s.

The National Archives in Washington, D.C., lists the Don as a historical monument, and it is one of three building landmarks used by the National Maritime Association on its maps and navigational aids for sailors. In April 1975 the Don was named to the National Register of Historic Places. An extensive renovation has been completed, and the palatial hotel glows throughout its ten stories with all its original elegance. (It has been given a Mobil four-star rating since 1978.)

The Don Ce Sar

The Don Ce Sar is at the southern end of the island of St. Petersburg Beach directly on the Gulf of Mexico. You can't miss it. It's the only thing around that is both huge and pink. The Don Ce Sar Beach Resort and Spa, 3400 Gulf Boulevard, St. Petersburg Beach, FL 33706; (813) 360–1881.

Directly south of St. Petersburg Beach is sprawling ◆ **Fort DeSoto Park,** a great place to get away from it all and spend some quiet time with the pelicans and great white herons. Its 900 acres, with more than 7 miles of waterfront and almost 3 miles of fine swimming beaches, ramble over five islands: Madeline Key, St. Jean Key, St. Christopher Key, Bonne Fortune Key, and the main island—Mullet Key.

Ponce De Leon anchored off Mullet Key during the summer of 1513 to clean the barnacles off the bottom of his ship. He was interrupted by Indians who thought he had no business in their territory. In the skirmish that followed, the first white soldier known to be killed in North America died. Apparently Ponce De Leon didn't get the message that he was not welcome in the area. When he returned in 1521, he again fought with the Indians, this time receiving the wound that later caused his death in Havana, Cuba.

Construction of Fort DeSoto began in 1898 and was completed two years later. Its eight 12-inch mortars never fired a single shot at any enemy. The remains of this old fort graphically illustrated the then popular concept of harbor defense. Today it is an interesting relic of history, a good place to climb for a view of the surrounding sea.

Two islands provide a haven for campers, ancient oaks on the northern end of **Mullet Key** shade a lovely picnicking area, and lifeguards are on duty at the swimming beaches. There is a boat-launching ramp, two fishing piers, and a small restaurant and gift shop near the fort.

By car you can get to Fort DeSoto Park only by two toll bridges. This county park wants you to know, however, that the money goes to the State Road Department and not to the park; (813) 866–2484.

WESTERN INTERIOR

You'll get your exercise if you cover all forty acres of canopies, stalls, and sheds at **Webster Flea Market,** one of the largest flea markets in the Southeast. It's hard to believe this all started in 1937 as a one-shed farmers' produce auction. More than 1,700 vendors await you and your spare change. It's all here—from fine antiques, clothes, fresh produce, and homemade sausage to just plain junk. You'll be exhausted if you try to see everything there is to see, but you'll surely find at least one item you cannot live another day without. Open every Monday 8:00 A.M.–3:00 P.M. Webster Flea Market, P.O. Box 62, Highway 471, Webster, FL 33597. Located at 524 N. Market Boulevard; (904) 793–2021.

The **Dade Battlefield State Historic Site** is the picture of serenity now, but it was once drenched in blood. Here Indians, who were not pleased at the prospect of being evicted from their land, ambushed more than one hundred soldiers under the command of Major Francis L. Dade. The Dade Massacre, as it came to be known, touched off the Second Seminole War, a war that dragged on for seven years and became the country's costliest Indian war. While visiting the small museum and reading the markers along the nature trail, you'll have a chance to ponder the events of December 28, 1835. Dade Battlefield Historic Site, P.O. Box 938, Bushnell, FL 33513. Located southwest of Bushnell off U.S. 301; (904) 793–4781.

GULF COAST

If you haven't looked a manatee in the eye lately, you'll never have a better opportunity than at ◆ **Homosassa Springs Wildlife Park.** You may pay a visit to these gentle mammals while walking under water (and staying nice and dry) at Fish Bowl Spring.

Besides the lovable manatees, you'll see more than thirty-four varieties of fish, both saltwater and freshwater species. Feeding time at Gator Lagoon will cure you of thinking you can outswim a hungry gator. A fish is hooked to a wire and skimmed across the pool with alligators in hot pursuit. Wow! Be sure to take the nature cruise and stroll the trails. Open 9:00 A.M.–5:30 P.M. Located just west of U.S. 19. Homosassa Springs, 9225 W. Fishbowl Drive, Homosassa Springs, FL 34448; (904) 628–2311 (recorded message); (904) 628–5343 (park office).

Yulee Sugar Mill Ruins State Historic Site was once part of a thriving sugar plantation, the area's first known settlement made by a white man. David Yulee, a former U.S. senator, operated the mill for thirteen years beginning in 1851. He supplied the Confederate Army with sugar products until 1864 when a Union naval force burned Yulee's home to the ground. Interpretive signs will guide you through the partially restored sugar mill, the only antebellum structure of its kind in the country. Located in Homosassa on SR 490 southwest of U.S. 19. Write to Yulee Sugar Mill Ruins, c/o Crystal River State Archaeological Site, 3400 N. Museum Drive, Crystal River, FL 34428; (904) 795–3817.

And you thought Christmas came only once a year. Not at **Roger's Christmas House and Village,** which is open every day except December 25. You're welcome to browse the five houses of Christmas, which overflow with trees, wreaths, gifts, and the widest selection of ornaments in the country. Before long you are feeling festive. Next to the original house are Country Cottage, Magnolia House, Little House Under the Oak Tree, and Storybook Land with animated display figures. Open daily 9:30 A.M.–5:00 P.M. One block from the intersection of U.S. 98, SR 50A, and U.S. 41. Roger's Christmas House, 103 Saxon Avenue, Brooksville, FL 34601; (904) 796–2415.

◆ **Weeki Wachee Springs** is home to live mermaids as well as more traditional denizens of the deep. The unusual theatre is 16 feet below the surface of the spring (which is more than 137 feet deep) with glass windows for your viewing pleasure. Walk through lush tropical gardens and ride a **Wilderness River Cruise Boat,** which passes the Pelican Orphanage, a refuge for disabled sea birds. Weeki Wachee Springs, 6131 Commercial Way, Weeki Wachee, FL 34608. The theme park is on U.S. 19 South at the junction of SR 50; (904) 596–2062.

◆ **Tarpon Springs'** famous sponge industry began in the 1890s when John K. Cheyney launched his first sponge-fishing boat and began hooking sponges. In 1905 John Cocoris, a recent immigrant from Greece, introduced the diving techniques used to harvest sponges in the Mediterranean. The first Tarpon Springs sponger to try this method emerged after a ten-minute dive thoroughly convinced that these sponge beds could supply the whole world.

Word of the bountiful beds off Tarpon Springs spread to Greece, and soon whole families were packing up their lives and moving to the west coast of Florida. From their homeland they brought the colorful customs and traditional cuisine of the rich Hellenic culture.

The village prospered during the first forty years of the twentieth century as sponging grew to be a multimillion dollar business. Auctions held at the Sponge Exchange were lively affairs, and Tarpon Springs soon surpassed Key West as the country's main sponging center. But in the 1940s a mysterious disease known as the red tide decimated the sponge beds, and consumers began turning to synthetic sponges.

Today visitors fascinated by this Greek community stroll the **sponge docks,** which have been designated a National Historic Landmark. The Sponge Exchange has been taken over by boutiques and gift shops, but a few boats still return from sea with ropes of sponges drying in the rigging. The history of the sponge industry is recounted at **Spongeorama Exhibit Center,** and visitors may join a half-hour cruise featuring a sponge diving demonstration by a copper-helmeted diver.

Lining the docks are many Greek coffeehouses and restaurants where a meal of pastitso and baklava may be washed down with a glass of retsina wine. The Spongeorama Exhibit Center is at 510 Dodecanese Boulevard at the Sponge Docks; (813) 942–3771. Information on Tarpon Springs is available at the Greater Tarpon Springs Chamber of Commerce, 210 S. Pinellas Avenue, Tarpon Springs, FL 34689; (813) 937–6109.

The community still revolves around the church. **St. Nicholas Greek Orthodox Cathedral,** a fine example of neo-Byzantine architecture with icons, stained glass, and sculptured marble, was named for the patron saint of ships and seafaring men. The celebration of Epiphany, held each January 6, is a study in pomp and pageantry. The archbishop leads the colorful procession from the church to Spring Bayou, the site of the original settlement. There he releases a dove and tosses a large gold cross into the water. Young men dive for the sacred trophy, and the successful one receives a blessing, which is supposed to bring him a year of good luck. The community then funnels all its energies into singing and dancing. Especially during this Old World festival, Tarpon Springs seems more like a Mediterranean community than a Floridian one. The church is at 35 N. Pinellas Avenue; (813) 937–3540.

OCALA AREA

The Ocala area is a land of gently rolling hills, massive oaks bearded with Spanish moss, and sleek thoroughbreds gamboling in neatly fenced paddocks. This is the fastest-growing thorough-bred community in the world and is responsible for Florida's development, in less than half a century, as a major force in international racing and breeding.

The racing world sat up and took notice when Needles became the first Florida-bred to win the Kentucky Derby in 1956. Since then what started as a few converted cattle farms has grown to nearly 500 thoroughbred facilities. Marion County is now second only to Lexington, Kentucky, in concentration of ◆ **thorough-bred farms**.

Central Florida offers ideal conditions for raising superior thor-oughbreds. Year-round sunshine, mineral-rich water, and fertile pastureland have turned out to be a winning combination. Mild weather, with cold snaps rarely lasting more than a few days, plays an important role. Central Florida's extended springs and autumns flank a long summer. The absence of a harsh winter means that, rather than standing idle in their stalls, horses run free all year. Unlike its northern counterpart, a new Florida foal is usually out romping with its dam within hours of its birth.

The area is wonderfully scenic and many horse farms welcome visitors for self-guided tours, but the hours vary. Visitors are encouraged to pick up information at the Ocala/Marion Chamber of Commerce on 110 E. Silver Springs Boulevard, Ocala; or call (904) 629–8051.

Just east of Ocala is the ◆ **Ocala National Forest** with more than 300,000 acres of untamed springs, winding streams, and natural lakes. The southernmost national forest in the continen-tal United States, Ocala is a popular recreation area for canoeing, swimming, camping, hiking, picnicking, and hunting. Detailed maps of the forest may be obtained at the two ranger stations. USDA Forest Service, 325 John Knox Road, Suite F100, Tallahas-see, FL 32303. (904) 681–7265.

Although this is the largest area of sand pine in the world, with one of the largest deer herds in Florida, it is the clear, clean springs that steal the show. **Alexander Springs** pumps out sev-enty-six million gallons of 72-degree water each day of the year.

The spring here is so large that local scuba experts use it for new diver certification tests. Canoers use this run for an excursion into the unspoiled forest, and swimmers and sunbathers make good use of the large sand beach. Located in Ocala National Forest off CR 445.

Another favorite, **Juniper Springs,** contributes twenty million gallons to the local water supply. Besides swimming, the most popular activity is canoeing the 7-mile spring run. This campground is in such demand that reservations are not accepted, and accommodations are handled on a first-come basis. Located in Ocala National Forest on SR 40 just west of SR 19.

Salt Springs Recreation Area is on the shores of a beautiful natural spring, which empties into Lake George, the state's second-largest lake. The 5-mile spring run is ideal for canoeing, boating, and fishing; the spring boil is a mecca for swimmers and snorkelers. Located in Ocala National Forest on SR 19 about 21 miles north of SR 40, Salt Springs has complete camping facilities; (904) 685–2048.

Silver Glen Springs is a beautiful 1,000-acre camping area bordering a crystal clear spring. A good place to bird-watch, swim, boat, or fish. Located in Ocala National Forest off SR 19, 6 miles north of SR 40; (904) 685–3990.

Although Ocala's waterworks are impressive, they are literally just a drop in the region's overflowing bucket. Of the country's seventy-eight major springs, twenty-seven are in Florida. Its central section is literally riddled with them. Springs are classified according to volume—a major spring, one of first magnitude, produces 100 cubic feet of water a second, or more than sixty-four million gallons daily. The combined output from all 300 of Florida's known springs is eight billion gallons of water a day!

❿ **Silver Springs,** near Ocala, is the largest limestone artesian spring formation in the world. With an average output of 800 million gallons a day, the springs have the greatest long-term measured average flow of any freshwater group in Florida. No wonder early Indians considered them sacred and paid homage to them with elaborate ceremonies. Scientists have discovered evidence of human activity dating back a hundred centuries. Certainly this is one of Florida's oldest attractions.

Most of the earliest sightseers came by boat, although the 136-mile trip from Palatka involved several weeks poling along the tortuous Ocklawaha River. By the 1880s steamboats began regular trips from Palatka to the Springs carrying such notables as Mary Todd Lincoln, Harriet Beecher Stowe, and William Cullen Bryant. The expedition, a real breeze, took only two nights and a day. Visitors are rarely disappointed in this natural wonder. The limestone-filtered water in the deep blue pool inspired one early journalist to describe the springs as shining "like an enormous jewel." Phillip Morrell, a young man living at Silver Springs, invented the glass bottom boat to provide passengers their first fish-eye view of the aquatic world. Watching this everchanging panorama while gliding over the pellucid springs is still a favorite activity. Numerous movies and television shows, attracted by the extraordinary clarity, have done underwater filming in this location.

The luxuriant gardens and subtropical scenery on the 100-acre site add to the viewing pleasure. Other diversions at the springs include a petting zoo and a jungle cruise past a whole zoo's worth of exotic animals. You'll see giraffes, ostriches, camels, and a colony of monkeys descended from those used in the old Tarzan movies. Located just off I–75, 1 mile east of Ocala on SR 40. Open daily 9:00 A.M.–5:30 P.M. Florida's Silver Springs, P.O. Box 370, Silver Springs, FL 34489; (904) 236–2121.

EASTERN INTERIOR

The endangered manatees have long made ◆ **Blue Springs State Park** their winter home. These large mammals congregate in Blue Springs Run between November and March because the year-round 72-degree water offers a refuge from the chilly St. Johns River. You may view these large "sea cows" (adults weigh about a ton) from observation platforms along Blue Springs Run. Once common from the Carolinas to Texas, these gentle giants now survive only in Florida, and this is one of the few places you may observe them in their native habitat. A two-hour boat ride explores the St. Johns River and the area around Hontoon Island.

In 1872 the Thursby family built a big frame house on the top of an ancient snail shell mound. The house and grounds have been restored to look as they did in the 1880s when oranges grew in the yard and the family sent their crops to Jacksonville by steamboat. The park is a fine place to camp (six family vacation cabins available), canoe, swim, fish, picnic, snorkel, and scuba dive. Located 2 miles west of Orange City off I–4 and U.S. 17-92, the park opens at 8:00 A.M. and closes at sunset year-round. Blue Springs State Park, 2100 W. French Avenue, Orange City, FL 32763; (904) 775–3663.

The only way to reach ◆ **Hontoon Island State Park** is by boat. Luckily a daily ferry crosses the St. Johns River between the parking lot and the island. Of special interest is a 300-foot-long Timucuan Indian ceremonial mound. No vehicles are allowed. Besides being a sanctuary for the endangered bald eagle, this is a good place to fish, picnic, and camp in either tents or cabins. The park is open 8:00 A.M. to sunset daily year-round. Six miles west of DeLand off SR 44; (904) 736–5309.

Between Sanford and Longwood keep an eye out for the **Big Tree** marker. The country's largest bald cypress tree is less than a mile up the cutoff road. "The Senator" is 126 feet high with a diameter of 17½ feet and an estimated age of more than 3,000 years. Impressive! Big Tree Park is on General Hutchinson Parkway, Longwood, Florida. The Seminole County Parks and Recreation Department closes the gates at sunset. Free.

You are not going to believe there are this many cacti in the world until you tour the greenhouses at **Florida Cactus, Inc.,** in Plymouth. Is your idea of a cactus green? Take a good long look at the endless rows of red, yellow, and pink cacti. Check out the large map of the United States in which each state features a different variety of cactus.

You may buy (or just admire) dish gardens, colorful grafted cacti, cactus books, and a special fertilizer called cactus juice. The mailing address is Florida Cactus, Inc., P.O. Box 2900, Apopka, FL 32704. The greenhouse, at S. Peterson Road in Plymouth, Florida, is off U.S. 441. Turn off 441 south onto Boy Scout Boulevard. Follow the Florida Cactus signs to South Peterson Road. Open 7:30 A.M.–5:00 P.M. Monday through Friday and 7:30–11:30 A.M. on Saturday, closed Sunday; (407) 886–1833.

SOUTHWEST FLORIDA

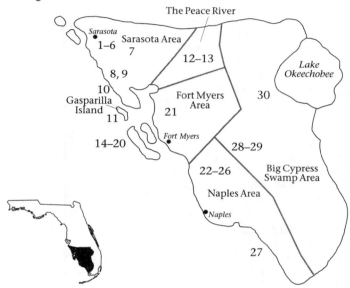

1. The John and Mable Ringling Museum of Art
2. Asolo Theatre
3. Circus Galleries
4. John Ringling's Home
5. Mote Marine Science Center
6. Marie Selby Botanical Gardens
7. Myakka River State Park
8. Basketville
9. Beaches around Venice
10. Palm Island
11. Gasparilla Island (Boca Grande)
12. Peace River
13. Canoe Outpost
14. Shell Factory
15. Sanibel Island
16. "Ding" Darling National Wildlife Refuge
17. Useppa Island
18. Cabbage Key
19. Thomas Edison's winter residence
20. Florida Power and Light Park
21. Koreshan State Historic Site
22. 1,000-foot fishing pier
23. Old Marine Market Place
24. Naples Beach Hotel and Golf Club
25. Conservancy Nature Center
26. Lighthouse Restaurant
27. Ten Thousand Islands
28. Corkscrew Swamp Wildlife Sanctuary
29. Big Cypress Swamp
30. Cypress Knee Museum

Southwest Florida

Sarasota Area

Aficionados of the arts feel right at home in Sarasota, which offers the appealing combination of sandy beaches and sophistication. Settled in 1842, the city's attributes were not really appreciated until it was "discovered" by a Chicago socialite in 1910. Wealthy and influential northerners followed, and in 1927 John Ringling decided this would be the ideal winter quarters for his circus. John and Mable Ringling were instrumental in making Sarasota what it is today.

"The Greatest Show on Earth" made a fortune for Ringling, who knew just what he wanted to do with his money. He built his dream mansion, poured millions into his art collections, and invested heavily in civic improvements for Sarasota. The Ringling enthusiasm was contagious, and the city became known as a mecca for the arts.

Today's proliferating art galleries and theatres are direct descendants of the circus king's munificence. ❖ **The John and Mable Ringling Museum of Art** gives visitors a chance to see a cultural complex that puts Florida on the fine arts map. Included are a museum of art with one of the most distinguished collections of Baroque art in the hemisphere, the ❖ **Asolo Theatre** (an eighteenth-century theatre imported in its entirety from Asolo, Italy), the ❖ **Circus Galleries,** and ❖ **John Ringling's Home.**

To call *Ca'd'Zan* (meaning House of John) simply Ringling's home doesn't quite do it justice. The thirty-two-room mansion on Sarasota Bay, patterned after the Doge's Palace on the Grand Canal in Venice, is one of America's great historic houses. Built in the 1920s at a cost of more than $1,500,000, this stately residence features a huge crystal chandelier from the lobby of New York's Waldorf Astoria Hotel and is elaborately furnished with art objects from around the world.

Although officially known as the House of John, Mable Ringling had a lot to say about the design. She insisted on including the tower of the old Madison Square Garden (where the circus regularly appeared) in the plans. The architects had some problems with the tower in combination with the Venetian Palace idea, but they gave in when Mable declared, "It is my house. I know what I want and that is that."

The Ringling Complex is open daily 10:00 A.M.–5:30 P.M. A restaurant is located near the Circus Museum. The complex is located on U.S. 41, 3 miles north of downtown Sarasota. The John and Mable Ringling Museum of Art, The State Art Museum of Florida, 5401 Bay Shore Road, Sarasota, FL 34243; (941) 395-5700.

Did you know that at least twenty-seven species of sharks inhabit the Gulf of Mexico off Sarasota? Were you aware that more than 600 species of fish and even more invertebrates live in Sarasota's Gulf and Bay waters? If you'd like to know more about these creatures of the deep, stop in at the ◆ **Mote Marine Science Center.** Guides will introduce you to the residents of thirty-six aquaria including "nibbles" the Nurse Shark. The sea horses and sea turtles are especially popular, as is the extensive shell collection. The Research Exhibits provide the inside scoop on current scientific projects and explain how this research applies to our lives. From downtown Sarasota follow CR 780 to St. Armands Circle, continue to New Pass Bridge Area, and look for directional signs. Open 10:00 A.M.–5:00 P.M. daily. Mote Marine Science Center, 1600 City Island Park, Sarasota, FL 33577; (800) 691–MOTE or (941) 388–4441.

Orchid lovers should spend some time browsing the extensive collection of tropical plants at the ◆ **Marie Selby Botanical Gardens.** This is the only public garden in the United States focusing on epiphytes, which are plants that grow on other plants. The research done here is vitally important because the tropical forests and jungles of the world are fast disappearing, and with them are going many rare and beautiful plants.

Eleven bay-front acres on the slender peninsula between Sarasota Bay and Hudson Bayou contain more than 20,000 colorful plants, including more than 6,000 orchids. Besides being a magnificent floral display, Selby is an internationally recognized center for botanical research, micropropagation, and plant identification.

Don't miss any of the fifteen garden areas, especially the Tropical Display House, the Bamboo Pavilion, the Waterfall Garden, the Banyan Grove, the Cactus and Succulent Garden, the award-winning Hibiscus Garden, and the Palm Grove. Also, be sure to visit the former Christy Payne Mansion, a unique example of eclectic Southern Colonial architecture, now serving as the Gardens' Museum of Botany and the Arts.

You'll enjoy strolling through the waterfront gardens and seeing the greenhouse abloom with elegant air plants. The gift and bookshop has tropical plants for sale along with books on everything you ever wanted to know about gardening. The gardens are located at U.S. 41 and South Palm Avenue, 4½ miles south of the Sarasota-Bradenton Airport. Open 10:00 A.M.–5:00 P.M. every day of the year. The Marie Selby Botanical Gardens, 811 S. Palm Avenue, Sarasota, FL. If you wish to have a guided tour, be sure to call ahead: (941) 366–5731.

◆**Myakka River State Park**—28,000 acres of river, lakes, marsh, hammocks, and prairies—is one of the country's outstanding wildlife sanctuaries and breeding grounds. A 5-mile drive through this scenic park will acquaint you with the overall features of the area, but to really experience its incredible diversity, why not rent a bike or, better yet, a canoe. Camping opportunities range from rustic cabins to a backpack trail that leads to six primitive camping areas.

Bird-watchers will feel that their time on the lakeshore birdwalk and observation platform has been well spent when they catch sight of a majestic bald eagle, great blue heron, sandhill crane, egret, or ibis.

Some 200 species of birds have been spotted in the park, and there are large rookeries. Board *Gator Gal,* the world's largest airboat, or the special **Safari Tram** (open December through June) for a scenic cruise. Both excursions are narrated by knowledgeable guides. The park is 14 miles east of Sarasota on SR 72. Open daily 8:00 A.M. to sunset; (941) 361–6511.

Basket lovers beware! ◆**Basketville** boasts the largest selection of baskets in the world, a claim you're sure to believe when you try to make up your mind to purchase something. You'll be swamped with choices that range from handcrafted baskets of white ash and red oak to a tremendous variety of permanent flowers, buckets, woodenware, wicker furniture accessories, and handmade imports from all over the world. Basketville is on U.S. 41, 4 miles south of Venice (4011 S. Tamiami Trail). Open Monday through Saturday 9:00 A.M.–8:00 P.M. and Sunday 9:00 A.M.–6:00 P.M. (941) 493–0007.

Because they are near the longest sloping continental shelf in the world, the ◆**beaches around Venice** are a fertile fossil hunting area, especially for shark teeth. Some of the teeth being washed ashore belong to creatures that have been extinct for millions of years. Put on your swimsuit and start scooping up sand in the shallow water. Keep a sharp eye out. Some teeth are very tiny. Free.

Folks who want to get off the beaten path love islands, but

Gator Gal **at Myakka River State Park**

77

they especially love bridgeless islands, islands without cars that are approached the way an island should be—by boat. That's one reason they love Palm Island.

This is the place for those who want to get away from the crowds, stroll the beach at sunrise, let the kids run free, snooze after lunch, and watch the evening sun sink into the Gulf of Mexico.

♠ **Palm Island** is a find! South of Sarasota on Florida's Southwest Gulf Coast, this 7-mile barrier island is north of Fort Myers and the islands of Sanibel and Gasparilla. The resort covers 2½ miles of this pristine island and consists of 200 individually owned beach villas and cottages, many available for rental. Minimum stay is two nights; the resort does not allow day-trippers.

If you have your own boat, fine. Palm Island is on the Intracoastal Waterway south of Lemon Bay a few minutes north of Gasparilla Pass near Charlotte Harbor. The channel entrance is midway between green marker "7" and red marker "8."

If you're yachtless, never fear. Park your car at the Palm Island Resort Reception Center's full-service marina and shift your mental gears to "no hassle." A bellman will take your bags and deliver them to your island villa. The resort launch leaves hourly for a twelve-minute cruise to Palm Island.

Step onto the island and feel the stress evaporate. Now your transportation is by island tram (which makes hourly runs around the resort), bike or electric golf cart (both available for rent), or footpower.

After you've beachcombed the glistening 2-mile beach for rare shells and prehistoric sharks' teeth, what is there to do? You may watch the dolphins play, bike or walk the resort's winding trails, go for a swim (five pools or the entire Gulf of Mexico), relax in the hydro spa, fish (rental boats, charter, or surf fishing), play tennis (eleven courts, lessons from the pro), watch the birds, snorkel, windsurf, waterbike, or explore Rum Bay by kayak or canoe.

The island recreation team keeps everyone (who wants to) jumping. There are playgrounds, displays, and programs at the nature center. An Island Kids Club sponsors activities ranging from nature walks, Kids' Movie Night, Kids' Olympics, sand castle construction, crafts and cooking classes, to shell and treasure hunts. Activities for adults run the gamut from nature walks to family bingo.

If being on Palm Island isn't off the beaten path enough, rent a bike and head south to Don Pedro Island State Recreation Area. Connected to Palm Island by two wooden bridges, Don Pedro is an easy 2-mile bike ride. The reward for your effort is a mile-long stretch (usually deserted) of gleaming white sandy beach. This is where loggerhead sea turtles come ashore during the summer to nest and lay eggs. The turtle nesting season is the reason you are asked to keep beach lights (including flashlights and beach fires) off from May 1 to October 31. Newborn turtles head for the brightest light, which in a natural state would be the Gulf of Mexico. If they head for artificial light inland, they become lost and eventually perish.

Florida beaches host the largest gathering of nesting sea turtles in the United States. Although these docile reptiles have been severely threatened by human activities in the past, enlightened citizens would like to see their numbers increase. For more information on sea turtles, contact the Florida Department of Natural Resources, Division of Marine Resources, Florida Marine Research Institute, 100 Eighth Avenue, SE, St. Petersburg, FL 33701. (813) 896–8626.

Accommodations in the Palm Island Resort are fully equipped one-, two-, or three-bedroom Old Florida–style villas with full kitchen, living and dining room, washer, dryer, and screened porch overlooking the Gulf of Mexico.

If your idea of a vacation does not include getting too well acquainted with the kitchen, saunter on down to the Rum Bay Restaurant, which is open for lunch and dinner. The chef serves a variety of burgers, salads, and sandwiches until 3:00 P.M.

Dinner is another story. You might want to whet your whistle with a Green Dolphin cocktail (vodka, blue Curacao, and sour mix) before diving into fresh char-grilled grouper. For those with hearty appetites, the island seafood sampler (crab cake, grilled shrimp, broiled freshwater snapper, and calamari rings) or the combination filet and lobster tail (two tails and a 5-ounce filet) will surely satisfy. The ribs are sensational, or, for a quick pick-me-up, try the shrimp pizza. Key lime pie provides the perfect finale.

Near the southern tip of the Cape Haze peninsula just south of Englewood, Palm Island is an easy ninety-minute drive from Fort Myers Airport. Those traveling south from Tampa should follow the signs for I–75 south to exit 34 (Englewood, North Port). Turn right on River Road. After crossing U.S. 41 continue to the STOP sign and turn right. Continue about 7 miles to Pine Street. Turn left on Pine and continue for another 7 miles. Palm Island Resort will be on the right side of CR 775.

Those traveling north from Fort Myers should follow signs for I–75 north to exit 32 (Toledo Blade Boulevard). Turn west on Toledo Blade, cross RT 41, and continue to the STOP sign; turn right onto SR 776 and follow it for 15 miles to CR 775. Turn left and continue 5½ miles until you come to Palm Island Resort on the right.

Palm Island Resort, 7092 Placida Road, Cape Haze, FL 33946. (941) 697–4800 or (800) 824–5412.

As you leave Palm Island and pull out of the marina parking lot, turn right. Just down CR 775 (on the right) in Placida, you'll find the Fishery Restaurant with an expansive view of Gasparilla Sound. The family business has blended Old Florida with the new and put the emphasis where it should be—on fresh seafood.

Start with Gator Bites, tender fried alligator with key lime mustard, or try the famous Fishery Gumbo, a "mess of shrimp, crab, tomato, and okra." You can't miss with a Thunderation Platter (broiled grouper, shrimp, oysters, and scallops) or a Snapper Melt with tomato and honey mustard on marble bread. Finish your feast off with Key Lime Cheesecake or Orange (!) Key Lime Pie. Chocoholics will be totally happy with the Ultimate Turtle Haagen-Dazs Ice Cream Pie. The Fishery Restaurant, P.O. Box 39, Placida, FL 33946. (813) 697–2451.

If you enjoyed the hand-painted silks in the Fishery Restaurant, drop by the Margaret Albritton Gallery next door to browse more of this artist's original paintings and crafts. Greg Albritton did the wooden fish you saw in the restaurant. His work is in the Placida Cove (the pink and green building) along with crafts, clothing, jewelry, and other fun things.

GASPARILLA ISLAND

Pristine shell-strewn beaches, fragrant tropical flowers, and not a single traffic light on the entire island. Year-round sunshine tempered by breezes from the Gulf. Best tarpon fishing in the world. Streets that make a statement: Dam If I Know, Dam If I Care, and Dam If I Will. Welcome to ◆ **Gasparilla Island** or, as it is better known (for its main community), **Boca Grande.**

Gasparilla, approximately an hour's drive south of Sarasota, is one of a string of barrier islands scattered along southwest Florida's coast between Tampa and Fort Myers. Bordered on the west by the Gulf of Mexico, on the north by Little Gasparilla Pass, on the east by Charlotte Harbor, and on the south by Boca Grande Pass, the island is accessible by toll bridge or boat.

Boca Grande (Spanish for "big mouth") Pass, one of Florida's deepest natural inlets, accounts for its early history. Calusa Indians were drawn to its rich fishing grounds. Railroads that once carried phosphate mined in central Florida to the island's deep water harbor later transported distinguished guests for the winter season.

Today Boca Grande's population of nearly 800 more than triples during winter and spring. Visitors come for their own reasons, which range from exhilarating angling to somnolent afternoons under a palm tree.

No wonder Katharine Hepburn adores the ice cream in Boca Grande. At one time a handwritten note of hers posted in the **Loose Caboose** declared: "That ice cream is perfect—Wow!" Of course, you might not see it amidst the general accumulation of stuff—the fuzzy alligator wearing sunglasses, the antique vacuum cleaner on the wall, or the sign: STOP—LOOK—LISTEN—PROCEED WHEN TRAIN IS COMING.

Not to worry. There hasn't been a train here in years. The preferred transportation is by bicycle, and the bike path extends the length of this lush, 7-mile sliver of land. Lots of folks prefer parking their cars and relying solely on pedal power. Better for the blood pressure. Come to think of it, the entire island of Gasparilla is good for the blood pressure. Stash the alarm clock. You'll know when the sun emerges and when it slips into the Gulf. If you must know how long it takes to reach tournament-size tarpon, the answer is "not long." Listen up: The major sounds on this tranquil island are gulls calling or maybe the soft whisper of a dolphin breathing.

The Boca Grande Chamber of Commerce consists of a personable woman in the Chamber of Commerce office who'll give you a map and offer to "tell you anything you want to know." Where can you get the best breakfast in town? **Loons on a Limb.** Best undiscovered art gallery? Next to the Theater Restaurant. Best place to have your *Wall Street Journal* delivered? Fugates. Best local news source? *The Boca Beacon* ties with the local librarian. The best grouper sandwich? **Millers Marina.** The best onion rings? Also at Millers. The best clams? The killer Cajun Clam Strips at—where else?—the **Casual Clam Cafe.** The best dinner? Local sentiment favors the **Temptation,** with **The Pink Elephant** (islanders call it "The Pink") a close second.

Apparently, the folks staying in the grand old **Gasparilla Inn** are quite happy with their fare, or they wouldn't return with such astonishing regularity. In 1911 when the twenty-room inn was newly opened and so empty it echoed, the first inquiry came from a socially prominent Bostonian. Before granting a reservation, the manager asked her to wire both a social and a bank reference. When the word got around that this hostelry catered to the "right" people, the right people appeared and stayed the season.

There are still two seasons on the island, the social season from November to April and the tarpon season from mid-April to July. The Gasparilla Inn, open from mid-December to June, has expanded to 150 rooms (with the addition of cottages) and boasts the only golf course (private) on the island.

What to do on Boca Grande? True beach lovers don't need anything more than dazzling white sand, a view of the distant horizon, and the gently lapping, Perrier-clear Gulf. Others enjoy shelling, birding, and all manner of water sports from fishing to sailboarding.

Grab your bike (rentals available) and wander the backroads. Island architecture, blessedly free of high-rises and time-shares, is an eclectic mix of Spanish-style stucco (note the community center and the Catholic church), elegant walled mansions of the rich and famous, and the more humble dwellings of fisherfolk.

Be sure to include the library—a distinctive pink stucco affair with coquina-rock walls, oversized cypress doors, and an intimate courtyard—in your ramblings. Browse the library's **shell collection** (donated by Henry Francis duPont) and ask for *Walking Tours on Boca Grande* or buy a copy at **Books in the Sand.**

A good place to walk is through the winding pathways of **Boca Bay** with its luxuriant landscaping, bridges, gazebos, and low-slung, generously latticed, wooden homes. This is the last residential community that can be built on the island, thanks to the conservation-minded 1980 Gasparilla Island Act, and it's satisfying to see its turn-of-the-century look blending so naturally into the island's easygoing style.

Explore at your own pace. If you're looking for local color, **Whidden's Marina** offers a double dose. Stop in **Our Lady of Mercy Chapel** to see the sixteenth-century Icon of Our Lady of Perpetual Help and other Old World treasures. Stroll down lanes canopied by banyans or hedged by scarlet hibiscus, and pause to admire a century-old gumbo-limbo tree. Breathe deeply of air perfumed by plumeria blossoms.

At day's end saunter down to Millers Marina and watch the fishing boats unload their catch or head for the restored 1890 lighthouse on the island's southern tip for a show that's always in season—a luminous bronze sun slipping into the Gulf of Mexico. For more information contact the Boca Grande Chamber of Commerce, Box 704, Boca Grande, FL 33921. (941) 964–0568.

THE PEACE RIVER

More shark teeth, some as large as your hand, can be found in the ✦ **Peace River.** In fact, a canoe trip down the pristine Peace can provide you with one of your very best off-the-beaten-track experiences in the entire state. Florida's most uninhabited waterway winds its tranquil way (too shallow for motorboats) from a source in central Florida's Green Swamp to the Gulf of Mexico. Once the Peace marked the boundary between Indian territory to the east and white settler's land to the west.

Every bend in the river is a movie set of palmettos, pine, cypress knees, and long strands of gray Spanish moss hanging from the gnarled limbs of live oaks. Wildflowers line the banks and large waterbirds stand in the shallows. You may spot armadillos, alligators, and deer. You will surely see cows that belong to the cattle ranches you paddle past. The perfectly clear water makes fossil finding easy, and there are many lovely spots to camp along the riverbanks.

Tailor your trip length to your own whims. Half-day trips are fun, but to really get in tune with this beautiful river, plan to spend several days. Put your canoe in at the bridge in Ft. Meade,

Our Lady of Mercy Chapel

Bowling Green, Wauchula, Zolfo Springs, Gardner, Brownsville, Arcadia, or Nocatee.

The friendly folks at ✦ **Canoe Outpost** will help select the right trip for you, answer all your questions, and provide whatever you need to be comfortable and safe. They can furnish either transportation upstream or pick-up downstream, canoes, paddles, life cushions, all camping gear, coolers, and ice. Open year-round. Canoe Outpost (a mile northwest of Arcadia on CR 661), 2816 N.W. CR 661, Arcadia, FL 33821; (941) 494–1215.

FORT MYERS AREA

It's hard to resist such a huge collection of shells and coral. Pick out your own oyster (complete with pearl), examine rare shells from the seven seas, or select just the right piece of precious black coral. The ✦ **Shell Factory** has more than 70,000 square feet of temptations, which include a year-round Christmas shop, imported gifts, beachwear, and handmade moccasins. Quite a display! Located on U.S. 41 (N. Tamiami Trail) 4 miles north of Fort Myers. Open seven days a week 9:00 A.M.–6:00 P.M. (941) 995-2141.

◑ **Sanibel Island**'s fortunate location enables it to snare some of the ocean's most beautiful treasures. This pretty island has a well-deserved reputation as one of the three best shelling beaches on earth. (The others are in Africa and the Southwest Pacific.) Beachcombers take their hobby very seriously, pacing the shoreline with bodies bent in a position known locally as the "Sanibel Stoop."

Nearly half of the land on Sanibel and the adjoining island of Captiva has been preserved in its natural state. The most frequented sanctuary is the J. N. ◑ **"Ding" Darling National Wildlife Refuge,** named for a Pulitzer Prize–winning political cartoonist. Darling was an ardent conservationist before anyone ever heard the word ecology. This mangrove wilderness at the southern end of the Atlantic flyway is a way station for migrating ducks and shelters more than 200 varieties of birds including the endangered brown pelican. Viewing is best at sunrise or sunset. Visitors can drive, bike, or paddle winding canoe trails through the 5,000-acre refuge, which is laced with fishing streams and hiking trails. Visitor's Center open 9:00 A.M.–5:00 P.M. Call (941) 472-1100.

◑ **Useppa Island** has a beach that looks like it was yanked from the South Pacific and a swimming pool, tennis court, three-hole golf course, and deepwater marina. Best of all, it has a profusion of lush tropical vegetation—palms, royal poinciana, and massive banyans.

Useppa is considered the most beautiful island in the chain of islands in Pine Island Sound, but its air of serenity hides a tempestuous past. The Calusa Indians apparently found it appealing. Archaeologists claim this is the oldest continuously occupied landmass on the western Florida coast. (The Indians started piling up oyster shell mounds in 3500 B.C.)

For a while the notorious pirate, Jose Gaspar, held his favorite female captive here. (The run-of-the-mill ladies were kept in a group on the nearby island named for these unsavory goings on—Isle de las Captivas, now known as Captiva Island.) Joseffa was a headstrong sixteen-year-old who never did take to Gaspar.

85

He found this so withering to his ego that he chopped off her head. As you can imagine, this place has its share of ghost stories. (Local dialect changed *Joseffa* to *Useppa*.)

Streetcar tycoon John Roach bought Useppa in 1894, and publisher Barron Collier purchased it in 1912. Lots of rich and famous folks liked the combination of beauty and privacy that this tiny half-mile-long island afforded. Theodore Roosevelt, the Vanderbilts, the Rockefellers, Zane Grey, and Mae West stopped in from time to time, and the Izaak Walton Fishing Club was founded here. More recently Useppa served as the training ground for the Bay of Pigs invasion.

Neglect and deterioration threatened to scuttle the island's charm, but Gar Beckstead arrived just in time. In 1976 he purchased Useppa, moved his family there and started the long process of restoration. In his mission to recapture the past, Gar uncovered one historic treasure after another, including a bathtub full of signed tarpon scales. To stroll the east ridge's pink pathway to the old **Collier Inn** is to return to the era of the 1920s. Architecture is strictly controlled; new cottages are all white frame with lattice work and wide, screened porches to match their restored counterparts. No cars intrude on the quiet.

Today the island is run as a private club, but nonmembers are welcome to stay as long as a week on an "investigatory" visit. (Members arrive by boat or seaplane.) A wide range of rental accommodations are available. (941) 283–1061.

If you prefer a day trip, sign up to cruise on the *Lady Chadwick*. This 150-passenger, double-decked excursion boat takes passengers through scenic Pine Island Sound while the captain points out leaping dolphins and baby ospreys peering from nests on the channel markers. Choose from a Continental Breakfast Cruise, the Island Cruise, Sightseeing Cruise, or Dinner and Sunset Cruise. (941) 472–5300.

If your yacht is less than 100 feet, the marina can accommodate it. Useppa Island lies just 2 miles south of Boca Grande Pass at Marker 63 on the Intracoastal Waterway, midway between Naples and Sarasota on the southwest coast of Florida. Useppa Island Club, P.O. Box 640, Bokeelia, FL 33922; (941) 283–1061.

◆ **Cabbage Key** was once home of playwright and mystery novelist Mary Roberts Reinhart. Her house, built in 1938 on the highest point of the island, has been converted into **Cabbage**

Key Hide-Away Inn and Restaurant. One memorable feature of the inn is its "wallpaper" worth more than $22,000. Somewhere along the way, the guests started tacking one dollar bills to the walls, and signing them. Today these bills cover the ceilings, walls, and beams. Visitors get a kick out of locating "their" dollar when returning to Cabbage Key.

Cabbage Key is a popular watering hole with excellent docking facilities. You might want to explore the nature trails before dining on one of the outdoor porches. Accessible only by boat or seaplane, Cabbage Key is at Channel Marker 60 on the Intracoastal Waterway. Boats from three areas make the run to Cabbage Key. In the Charlotte Harbour area call (941) 639–0969. In the Fort Myers area call (941) 283–0015. In the Captiva area call (941) 472–7549. Cabbage Key is 5 miles south of Charlotte Harbour on the Intracoastal Waterway near marker #60. To reach the inn, call (941) 283–2278.

Fort Myers got its start as a military post during the Seminole Indian wars. Abandoned after a brief occupation by federal troops during the Civil War, the fort became the center of a tiny village reached, in those days, by boat. Majestic palm-lined avenues and a profusion of exotic flowers and fruit trees contribute to Fort Myers' tropical good looks.

Thomas Edison, who made his winter home here, imported 200 royal palms from Cuba in 1900, starting Fort Myers on its way to being known as a "City of Palms." Edison was a great promoter of Fort Myers and wanted to bestow the fruits of his genius on the local citizenry. Soon after perfecting the electric lamp, he offered to provide the entire city with electric streetlights. The town voted against the proposal when many expressed fear that the lights would keep the cows from getting a good night's sleep.

◆ **Thomas Edison's winter residence,** complete with chandeliers still burning with their original carbon filament bulbs, is open to the public. Edison held 1,096 patents, and many of his inventions are on display in the adjoining museum. You cannot help being impressed and inspired by this inventor's philosophy and achievements. Unusual plants and trees from the far corners of the globe flourish on his fourteen-acre homesite on the Caloosahatchee River. Open 9:00 A.M.–3:30 P.M. Monday through Saturday and 12:30–3:00 P.M. on Sunday. 2350 McGregor Boulevard, Fort Myers, FL 33901; (941) 334–3614.

Those who want to talk to the manatees should head for the ✦**Florida Power and Light Park** on SR 80 east of Fort Myers. The best viewing times are cold mornings, when these endangered "sea cows" are toasting their flippers in the warm waters of the power plant discharge. You may park your car alongside the lagoon south of SR 80. Open daily during daylight hours. Free.

The world is not flat, but round. Columbus proved it and you're sure, right? But can you really be sure that the earth isn't hollow, that life doesn't cover its inner walls and that the sun isn't actually in the center of this round sphere? If you find these thoughts intriguing, you should stop in at the ✦**Koreshan State Historic Site.**

Dr. Teed, a physician from Chicago, founded a **utopian commune** here in the later 1800s. The doctor brought a group with him from Chicago, but the movement never caught on, though some of his followers still publish a newspaper and magazine. For one thing, there were no children to carry the banner for Dr. Teed because he insisted everyone practice celibacy. You may visit the tropical garden and restored village of this pioneer settlement and learn how Dr. Teed went about proving his theories in the museum. This is also a good place to camp and canoe. Open daily 8:00 A.M. to sunset. Guided tours given according to seasonal demand. Take I–75, exit 19. Go 2 miles on Corkscrew Road to Junction 41, Estero, FL 33928; (941) 992–0311.

NAPLES AREA

The city of Naples caters to the upper crust with all the amenities money can buy, but it has not forgotten the less-well-heeled folk who have the run of its splendid 7-mile public beach and ✦ **1,000-foot fishing pier.** Shoppers will look a long time before finding such a marvelous assortment of shops. If your credit cards are suffering from lack of use, don't worry. Shopping in Naples is guaranteed to get them back in the swing of things.

Browsers are more than welcome at the ✦**Old Marine Market Place,** better known as Tin City. A carefully preserved part of Naples's past, now restored, awaits right on Naples Bay at 1200 Fifth Avenue S. This old-fashioned shopping bazaar was created from historic boat buildings connected by cobbled and planked river walks and comes complete with waterfront dining and open air markets. Don't miss the chic stores on Third Street and those marvelously posh emporiums on Fifth Avenue.

Longtime Naples resident Michael Watkins, general manager of the landmark Naples Beach Hotel and Golf Club, contends the best way to see this attractive area is by bike. His suggested route includes stops at Lowdermilk Park, the Conservancy Nature Center, Tin City, the restored historic Naples Depot, Cambier Park, Naples Fishing Pier, and the shops on Fifth Avenue and Third Street. In the process you'll pass through some gorgeous residential real estate. Bikes are available for rent at the hotel's front desk, along with complimentary bicycle maps. For information or reservations contact The ◆ **Naples Beach Hotel and Golf Club,** 851 Gulf Shore Boulevard N., Naples, FL 33940; (941) 261–2222.

The ◆ **Conservancy Nature Center** is, surprisingly, on a wooded fourteen-acre site right in the middle of Naples. The **Natural Science Museum** contains natural history, animal and marine displays, and participatory exhibits including a computer game, shell game, weather station, and marine life touch-tank. Be sure to stroll the two nature trails and visit the recuperating animals and birds (mostly eagles, hawks, and owls) in the **Animal Rehabilitation Clinic.** Tours of this center are given to the public Monday through Thursday 9:30 A.M.–noon and 1:00–4:30 in the afternoon. Half-hour powerboat trips run from November through March.

This private, nonprofit organization is dedicated to environmental protection, conservation, wildlife rehabilitation, nature education, and ecological research. The Conservancy Nature Center, 1450 Merrihue Drive, Naples, FL 33942 (1 block east of Goodlette Road). Open Monday through Saturday 9:00 A.M.–4:30 P.M. year-round. January through March open 1:00–5:00 P.M. on Sunday. Nature Center grounds open 8:30 A.M.–5:00 P.M., closed Sunday; (941) 262–0304. Free.

For casual waterfront dining (on outdoor picnic tables, if you wish), you should seek out the ◆ **Lighthouse Restaurant.** While peeling your shrimp and sipping a cold beer, you can watch the water-skiers zip by and the seagulls hover. (Please, heed the sign that asks you NOT to feed the birds. There's a very good reason for it.) The atmosphere is relaxed, the service friendly, and the jumbo sandwiches excellent. Open Sunday noon–9:00

P.M., all other days 11:00 A.M.–9:30 P.M. Lighthouse Restaurant, 9180 Gulf Shore Drive N., Naples, FL 33963; (941) 597-2551. Inexpensive to moderate.

Thirty miles to the south of Naples are the ◆ **Ten Thousand Islands.** This maze of mangrove islands teeming with fish and bird life is best approached with a guide. Conducted tours leave from Everglades City, the entrance to the western portion of Everglades National Park. This is literally the jumping-off place, because access to the wilderness is by water.

One of the most satisfying ways to explore these islands, if insect repellent is at hand, is by canoe. To glide quietly by an egret rookery, to listen to the beat of many wings as flocks pass overhead, and to watch the evening sun beam a path of orange across a silent sea is to know Florida at its very best.

Sightseeing tours into the Ten Thousand Islands region and the mangrove swamps of the northwestern Everglades leave from the Gulf Coast Ranger Station between November 1 and May 1. For information about boat tours (available year-round) and boat rentals at the Gulf Coast Ranger Station, write the concessioner at Everglades National Park Boat Tours, P.O. Box 119, Everglades City, FL 33929, or call Everglades National Park: (941) 695-2591.

BIG CYPRESS SWAMP AREA

◆ **Corkscrew Swamp Wildlife Sanctuary,** maintained by the National Audubon Society, is an 11,000-acre preserve with a dwindling population of wood storks. These rare large birds, dangerously close to extinction, are definitely worth the trip. The most interesting time to visit is from December through March when the storks nest and breed. Their breeding is timed so that young storks are raised when food is plentiful (which depends entirely on receding water levels to concentrate the fish). An unexpected rainstorm at the wrong time of year can mess up the whole process. (A single family of wood storks requires 440 pounds of food per breeding season!) The frantic activity of the nesting season is something to see. The male gathers the sticks for the nest, the female arranges them, and young storks kick up quite a racket.

The sanctuary also protects the largest stand of virgin bald cypress trees in the country. A boardwalk trail (1¾ miles long) winds through this primeval forest of huge trees, some more than 700 years old! An illustrated self-guiding tour booklet describes plants and animals, and there are members of the staff along the way to answer questions. You'll see lots of birds, turtles, and alligators along with a variety of lush plant life.

Take a lunch to eat in the pleasant picnic area, because there isn't any place nearby to buy so much as a snack. The sanctuary is located 21 miles east of Naples, 14 miles from Immokalee and 21 miles from U.S. 41. Go east on Immokalee Road (CR 846). Look for Sanctuary Road. The entrance is at the end of Sanctuary Road. No pets admitted, and overnight camping is not permitted within sanctuary boundaries or in parking area. The visitor center and boardwalk are open daily 8:00 A.M.–5:00 P.M.; 7:00 A.M.–5:00 P.M. December through April. For information write: Chief Naturalist, Corkscrew Swamp Sanctuary, 375 Sanctuary Road, Naples, FL 33964, or call (941) 657–3771.

Corkscrew Swamp Sanctuary is at the northern end of ◆ **Big Cypress Swamp,** a vast wilderness area administered by the National Park Service. You may explore the swamp by car on Alligator Alley (I–75) and Tamiami Trail (U.S. 41), which are connected by SR 29. The fascinating Loop Road (CR 94) from 40-Mile Bend to Monroe Station is only paved for 8 miles. Be careful on unpaved roads as they can be dusty and rough or, worse, muddy, as in stuck-in-the-mud.

Approximately one-third of Big Cypress is covered by cypress and the rest is given over to prairies of saw grass, mixed hardwood hammocks, marshes, and estuarine mangrove forests. You may also see alligator, wild turkey, deer, mink, bald eagle, ibis, heron, egret, and wood stork. The Oasis Visitor Center is on Oasis Ranger Street. The Oasis Ranger Station is 55 miles east of Naples on U.S. 41 in the Preserve. For information write: Park Superintendent, Big Cypress National Preserve, Star Route Box 110, Ochopee, FL 33943, or call (941) 695–4111 or (from Naples) 263–3532.

Those continuing north on SR 29 will eventually come to Palmdale and the ◆ **Cypress Knee Museum.** Tom Gaskins experiments in controlled cypress knee growth, and some of his creations are not to be believed. You'll be fascinated by the museum, which is built around the world's largest transplanted cypress tree. Save the best for last—a ½-mile catwalk stroll through a cypress swamp, cabbage palm and oak hammock, and bayhead. The sign in front of the museum assures visitors that it was built by a "selfish reactionary" without any help from "city, county, state or federal government" and that it contains "souvenirs of a time before civilization covered the United States." Cypress Knee Museum is 1 mile south of Palmdale, near the junction of U.S. 27 and SR 29. Open daily 8:00 A.M. to sundown. (941) 675-2951.

SOUTHEAST FLORIDA

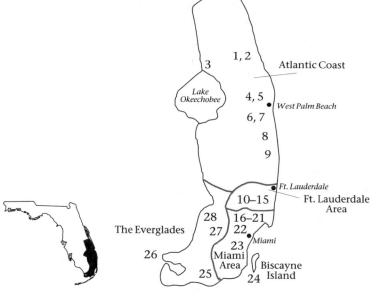

3

1, 2

Atlantic Coast

Lake Okeechobee

4, 5

● *West Palm Beach*

6, 7

8

9

Ft. Lauderdale

10–15

Ft. Lauderdale Area

The Everglades

28

27

16–21

22

23 ● *Miami*

Miami Area

26

25

24

Biscayne Island

1. Elliott Museum
2. Gilbert's Bar House of Refuge
3. Lake Okeechobee
4. Jonathan Dickinson State Park
5. Jupiter Lighthouse
6. Henry Morrison Flagler Museum
7. Norton Museum of Art
8. Morikami Park, Museum and Gardens
9. Cap's Place
10. *Jungle Queen* Riverboat
11. Stranahan House
12. Museum of Discovery and Science
13. Museum of Art
14. Flamingo Gardens

15. Davie Rodeo Arena
16. Cloisters of the Monastery of St. Bernard de Clairvaux
17. Miami Beach Historic Architectural District
18. Eden Roc Resort and Spa
19. Little Havana
20. Vizcaya Museum and Gardens
21. The Barnacle
22. Parrot Jungle
23. Monkey Jungle
24. Biscayne National Park
25. Everglades National Park
26. Sightseeing boats
27. Shark Valley
28. Miccosukee Indian Village

Southeast Florida

Atlantic Coast

Sebastian Inlet State Recreation Area is now an ocean playground, but you would have a hard time telling that to the survivors of the fleet of ships that went down here in 1715. Spanish galleons, loaded with gold and silver, were pummeled by a terrible storm before they sank to the bottom of the sea. At the **McLarty Museum** you'll see artifacts of the Ais Indians, as well as exhibits and dioramas on the Spanish treasure. The salvage efforts, both historic and recent, are a story in themselves.

Located in Sebastian Inlet on SR A1A about midway between Melbourne and Vero Beach, the area offers outstanding fishing and camping. The time to beachcomb for ancient pieces of eight is right after a storm. You'll need a lot of luck, but it's not impossible. Sebastian Inlet State Recreation Area, 9700 South A1A, Melbourne Beach, FL 32951; (407) 984–4852. The museum is open 10:00 A.M.–5:00 P.M. daily year-round.

How can you resist a look at the **Driftwood Inn** in Vero Beach, especially when you hear how this rickety looking "Menagerie of Monstrosities" got started? Some residents remember Waldo Sexton creating his architectural extravaganza from driftwood in the 1930s. He would pace up and down the beach shouting instructions to crews who were working without plans. As a result nothing seems to be square or level, but does this place ever have character!

Sexton filled his inn with a conglomeration of objects ranging from ships' wheels to early Italian chests and a vast collection of bells. Sexton used to love to show off his collection to visitors and regale them with tales of how he acquired each piece. When one woman took the tour two days in a row, she was amazed to discover these delightful stories had totally changed from one day to the next. When she pointed out the discrepancy to Waldo, he replied, "Madame, I'd rather be a liar than a bore any day."

Lunch at Waldo's, among the antiques, is fun. On a nice day you can eat by the pool overlooking the ocean. A menu that announces "We'll a la mode anything" can't really miss. Try the Cajun grouper sandwich or the China Coast salad. (407)

231–7091. The Driftwood Inn Resort is at 3150 S. Ocean Drive, Vero Beach, FL 32960; (407) 231–0550. Lunches are inexpensive. The ✦**Elliott Museum** is really more like a tiny town. Besides a dozen Early American shops brought from Salem, Massachusetts, there are antique automobiles, motorcycles, Seminole artifacts, a shell collection, and a contemporary art gallery. The museum was built in 1961 by Sterling Elliott's son to house his father's inventions, which included the first addressing machine, a knot-tying machine, and the original quadracycle. On Hutchinson Island's Ocean Boulevard near Stuart. Open daily 11:00 A.M.–4:00 P.M.; (407) 225–1961.

The ✦**Gilbert's Bar House of Refuge** (1875) is the last of eleven original structures built along the coast in the 1800s to rescue shipwrecked sailors. This National Historic Site perched on a rocky cliff contains a sea aquarium and a boathouse with early lifesaving equipment. The House of Refuge is on Hutchinson Island near Stuart. Follow signs that take you through Indian River Plantation. The entrance is south of the plantation. Open daily except Monday 11:00 A.M.–4:00 P.M.; (407) 225–1875.

If you'd like to view water traffic negotiating the 14-foot St. Lucie Locks, drive 8 miles southwest of Stuart on SR 76 for a look.

Bass fishermen should head for ✦**Lake Okeechobee,** about 40 miles inland, which is the second-largest lake wholly within the United States. It might encourage you to know that more than 3,500,000 pounds of fish (including both sport and commercial catches) are caught here every year. Take your pick of fishing camps; they are all over the place.

Back on the coast, **Blowing Rock Preserve** on Jupiter Island is worth a ten-minute walk through a pine forest. When a stiff wind is coming out of the northeast, the surf surges through holes in the rocks to create spectacular geysers.

It's only 85 feet high, but in Florida they call it a mountain even if it is only an overgrown sand dune. Add a 25-foot observation tower to Hobe Mountain in ✦**Jonathan Dickinson State Park** and you have a good view of ocean and the surrounding woodlands.

The park was named for a Quaker who was shipwrecked nearby in 1696, discovered by Indians, and survived all sorts of traumas before getting his wife and baby safely home to Philadelphia. His journal provides valuable insight into early Florida.

An exciting way to see the park is a trip down the Loxahatchee River to Trapper Nelson's camp. The Loxahatchee is the only National Wild and Scenic River in the state of Florida, and you really ought to experience it. Take the thirty-passenger pontoon boat, **Loxahatchee Queen,** or rent a canoe and paddle past the alligators and bald eagles to Trapper Nelson's. The boat ride takes almost two hours; if you paddle yourself, count on three hours. Alas, the legendary Trapper Nelson is no longer with us, but a ranger will fill you in on some of his eccentricities.

A wide range of activities includes fishing (both salt- and freshwater), boating, camping, and bicycling. The park, on U.S. 1, 6 miles north of Jupiter, is open 8:00 A.M. to sunset year-round, but if you're interested in the boat trip, call because it does not go every day. Jonathan Dickinson State Park, 16450 S.E. Federal Highway, Hobe Sound, FL 33455; (407) 546–2771.

In Jupiter, the 105-foot redbrick ❖**Jupiter Lighthouse** is one of the oldest (1860) lighthouses on the Atlantic coast. Still functioning, it is operated by the Coast Guard as a navigational aid. The Lighthouse, beside Jupiter Inlet, provides a fine view of the Gulf Stream. Open 10:00 A.M.–5:00 P.M. Tuesday through Friday and 1:00–5:00 P.M. Saturday and Sunday. Call (407) 747–6639.

A great place to contemplate the Jupiter Lighthouse and watch a steady stream of boats passing at the same time is **Harpoon Louie's.** You may eat inside or, better yet, on the expansive deck. Louie puts together a memorable selection of salads and sandwiches, and his hot dog steamed in beer is not bad, either. For dinner you can't do better than seafood Wellington or fresh fish char-grilled on open coals with a liberal dose of garlic butter sauce. The restaurant is open 11:00 A.M.–10:00 P.M. seven days a week. Easy to find, it's right across from the Jupiter Lighthouse. Prices range from inexpensive to moderate. In Jupiter; (407) 744–1300.

Burt Reynolds is a local boy who put Jupiter on the map while making a name for himself. You may visit his horse ranch, feedstore, gift shop, museum, and petting zoo a short drive from town. A number of movies have been made here. Walk down memory lane among movie pictures and memorabilia in the Burt Reynolds Museum and tour the 160-acre ranch including a sound stage and actual movie sets.

The gift store has a good selection of hats, boots, belts, and clothing. Photographs of Burt Reynolds starring in numerous films and plays, autographed photos of other stars, and Burt's awards adorn the walls.

The feedstore offers dog food in great quantity, and the neatly kept petting zoo has a bunch of friendly animals eagerly awaiting your handful of food. The petting zoo is free. The ranch, open seven days a week 10:00 A.M.–5:00 P.M., offers daily tours and is 2 miles west of the Florida Turnpike and I–95 on Jupiter Farms Road. Look for fancy white wrought iron gates with the initials BR. Call (407) 746–0393.

The Palm Beach area was developing slowly until Henry Flagler pushed his famous railroad south. With the railroad's arrival in 1894 and the grand hotels that Flagler built, Palm Beach quickly established, and still holds, a reputation as an enclave for the ultra wealthy. When Flagler planned his own Palm Beach home, he chose the architectural firm that had built the New York Public Library and the U.S. Senate Office Building. Described in the press as "more wonderful than any palace in Europe" and costing $4 million to build and furnish in 1901, Whitehall is a showcase that has been marvelously refurbished as the ❖ **Henry Morrison Flagler Museum.** The multimillionaire's private railroad car is on display, as are treasures collected from all over the world. The mansion provides a glimpse into the era before income taxes and sets a new standard for the term opulent. The museum is on Whitehall Way, off Coconut Row, in Palm Beach. The Henry Morrison Flagler Museum, P.O. Box 969, Palm Beach, FL 33480. Open Tuesday through Saturday 10:00 A.M.–5:00 P.M. and Sunday noon–5:00 P.M.; (407) 655–2833.

The ❖ **Norton Museum of Art** has a reputation as one of the foremost small museums in the United States. Outstanding collections include modern French and American paintings along with some 200 Chinese objects including archaic jades and Buddhist sculpture. The gallery is at 1451 S. Olive Avenue, West Palm Beach, FL 33401. Open Tuesday through Saturday 10:00 A.M.–5:00 P.M.,Thursday evening until 8:00 P.M., and Sunday 1:00–5:00 P.M.; (407) 832–5194. Free.

You may never have heard of George Morikami, but you will be impressed with his life story and the ❖ **Morikami Park, Museum and Gardens** he donated. This humble pineapple farmer lived in a modest trailer and never stopped working his fields even though he amassed considerable wealth. You will be asked to remove your shoes (paper slippers provided) before entering the museum, where individual rooms are devoted to the tea ceremony, depict a traditional Japanese bedroom, or contain photographs of George Morikami and the local Japanese farming community. The tranquil gardens contain bonsai displays. The Morikami Museum of Japanese Culture, 4000 Morikami Park Road, Delray Beach, FL 33446. Open Tuesday through Sunday 10:00 A.M.–5:00 P.M.; (407) 495–0233.

Did Architect Addison Mizner ever leave his mark on Boca Raton! In 1918 the forty-five-year-old, suffering from heart and lung ailments, came to Florida to die. As restless as he was eccentric, he became bored with dying and began designing homes for the super rich. He parlayed his profits into a fortune by wheeling and dealing in real estate and then tackled his real ambition— building a dream city.

He designed The Cloister to be a hotel worthy of being the centerpiece for this splendid project and held a grand opening in February 1926. At the time it was the most expensive 100-room hotel ever built; the style of architecture has been summed up as "Bastard-Spanish-Moorish-Romanesque-Gothic-Renaissance-Bull-Market-Damn-the-Expense." But Florida went quickly from boom to bust and the hotel closed after a single season. Mizner's extravagant vision fizzled, but his pink wedding-cake hotel was destined to play many roles over the years, including one as a World War II barracks.

Today the **Boca Raton Hotel and Club,** its original splendor intact, thrives in its reincarnation as a premier resort. The hotel is on Camino Real between U.S. 1 and SR A1A and is on the Intracoastal Waterway across from its seaside extension, the Boca Beach Club. Boca Raton Hotel and Club, 501 East Camino Real, Boca Raton, FL 33432; (407) 395–3000.

Care to eat where Winston Churchill, Franklin D. Roosevelt, and the Vanderbilts once dined? If that list doesn't impress you, how about Casey Stengel and Jack Dempsey? Both notables and nonnotables have been flocking to ❖ **Cap's Place** for a long time because of its excellent fresh fish.

Back in the 1920s, this group of wooden shacks attached to an old barge was floated up the Intracoastal Waterway from Miami to its present location on Cap's Island. Once a center for rum-running and gambling, the restaurant has cleaned up its act, if not its ramshackle appearance, and serves dinner daily from 5:00 P.M. The trick is knowing how to get there. In Lighthouse Point follow N.E. Twenty-fourth Street toward the ocean. Soon you'll see official looking signs leading the way to Cap's Place. You'll end up in a parking lot. If the boat isn't there, don't worry. It'll arrive soon. After a brief boat ride to the island, a "Welcome to Cap's" sign hoves into view. The building looks pretty run-down, but say hello to the pelicans roosting in the nearby trees and press on.

Inside you'll find a rattlesnake skin on the wall measuring more than six feet and a sign that says HELP PRESERVE WILDLIFE, THROW A PARTY AT CAP'S. The floors are uneven, but the food is good. You can't miss with a stone crab appetizer (in season), hearts of palm salad, the catch of the day, and Key lime pie. Entrees range from moderate to expensive. The boat ride is free, but tips are appreciated on the return trip. Call (954) 941–0418.

FORT LAUDERDALE AREA

Pompano Beach Air Park is the winter home of the *Stars and Stripes,* one of four touring dirigibles in the world. The blimp is 192 feet long, 55 feet wide, and 59 feet high. Powered by small engines, it has a cruising speed of 35 mph and can operate eight hours a day for a week on the same amount of fuel it takes to taxi a big jet out to the runway for takeoff. The new Visitor Center is open to the public November through May. Sorry, you can't take a ride, but you will get a good closeup look at this huge flying machine. At 1500 N.E. Fifth Avenue on the west side of Pompano Air Park; (954) 946–8300.

One way to glimpse Fort Lauderdale's glittering waterways is by cruising on the ✦*Jungle Queen* **Riverboat.** Daily sightseeing cruises at 10:00 A.M. and 2:00 P.M. (dinner cruise at 7:00 P.M.) go up New River and by Millionaires Row with a stop off at Indian Village to see birds, monkeys, and real live alligator wrestling. You'll learn something about the history of the area, where the cruise liners in Port Everglades are heading, who lives where, and how they made their money. Leaves from Bahia Mar Yachting Center, 801 Seabreeze Boulevard, Fort Lauderdale, Fl 33316; (954) 462–5596.

Speaking of cruises, thousands of people cruise to exotic ports of call from **Port Everglades.** More than twenty cruise lines depart from six ultramodern terminals. This is the deepest port between Norfolk and New Orleans and serves more five-star cruise ships than any other port in the nation. You'll get a good view of Port Everglades activity from the S.E. Seventeenth Street Causeway Bridge.

You can watch manatees and tropical fish basking in the warmth of the Port Everglades Power Plant's water discharge from the parking and picnic area on Eisenhower Boulevard and S.E. Twenty-sixth Street.

One of Fort Lauderdale's worst-kept secrets is a restaurant that doesn't advertise and is appropriately named **By Word of Mouth.** Before you are seated, you are shown all the evening's selections and the host or hostess describes the ingredients and methods of preparation. You may select sun-dried tomato and pesto pâté, a salad of smoked turkey with dried cherries and hazelnuts, New Mexican cornbread salad, Key West lobster with Amaretto cream, and then top the whole thing off with a house favorite, chocolate raspberry cake.

By Word of Mouth is at 3200 N.E. Twelfth Avenue in Fort Lauderdale. The word is out. (Being featured in *Gourmet Magazine* took care of that.) You'd better make a reservation; (954) 564–3663. Expensive.

The ◆**Stranahan House** is a gem. When Frank Stranahan came to take charge of the New River overnight camp in 1893, it was the only outpost on a road between Lake Worth and Lemon City (now North Miami). By the late 1890s, Stranahan's trade with the Seminole Indians was at its peak and winter tourism was in its infancy.

Love and marriage entered his life when the first teacher arrived at the new settlement. The couple's restored store/home of classic Florida frontier design is the oldest existing structure in Broward County. The Stranahan House (off Las Olas Boulevard, at the New River tunnel) is at 335 S.E. Sixth Avenue, Fort Lauderdale, FL 33301. Open for tours Wednesday through Saturday 10:00 A.M.–4:00 P.M. and Sunday 1:00–4:00 P.M. Call (954) 524–4736.

Ever dream of becoming an astronaut or a musical genius? The ◆**Museum of Discovery and Science** provides the opportunity to explore these notions along with many other mysteries of science. Exhibit areas are displayed over two floors including Florida EcoScapes, a bi-level ecology mountain complete with live animal and plant species; Space Base, a simulation of the weightlessness of space on a Manned Maneuvering Unit; Kid-Science, featuring its own whimsical musical staircase; and Choose Health, an interactive examination of how nutrition and controlled substances affect the human body. Play a game of virtual volleyball. Spin like a "human hurricane." Lift a 500-pound weight with a giant lever. Program a robot. You can do it all at Gizmo City, one of the museum's exciting permanent exhibits. One of the museum's most popular attractions is the five-story-high Blockbuster **IMAX Theater** with a larger-than-life technique that allows viewers to "feel" the momentum of high-flying special effects. The Museum of Discovery and Science and its IMAX Theater are at 401 S.W. Second Street on downtown Fort Lauderdale's historic Riverwalk. Exhibit hours are 10:00 A.M.–5:00 P.M. Monday through Saturday and noon–5:00 P.M. Sunday. It is the northern anchor of Broward County's Arts and Science District across from the Broward Center for the Performing Arts. (954) 467–6637.

Fort Lauderdale's multimillion-dollar ✦**Museum of Art** is a real prize. Some have called its astonishing twentieth-century collection "unsettling" and "disturbing," but none has denied its vitality. The impressive fan-shaped museum features six distinctive exhibition spaces, a sculpture terrace, gift shop, and art library. It contains the largest collection of ethnographic material in Florida encompassing Oceanic, West African, pre-Columbian, and American Indian art.

The museum is at One East Las Olas Boulevard, Fort Lauderdale, FL 33301. Open Tuesday 10:00 A.M.–9:00 P.M., Wednesday through Saturday 10:00 A.M.–5:00 P.M., and Sunday noon–5:00 P.M., closed Monday and all national holidays. Parking is available at the Municipal Parking facility on S.E. First Avenue that borders the museum on the east. Ask for hours of free public tours. Call (954) 525–5500.

The largest tree in Florida, a cluster fig 49 feet in circumference and 108 feet tall, keeps right on growing at ✦**Flamingo Gardens.** That's just the beginning. There are also sixty acres of botanical gardens, an Everglades wildlife sanctuary, a tram ride through citrus groves, alligators, and peacocks. This is your chance to see a sausage tree, an African tulip tree, and a gumbo limbo, along with other exotic plants and trees. West of Hollywood off SR 84 at 3750 Flamingo Road, Fort Lauderdale, FL 33330. Open 10:00 A.M.–6:00 P.M. daily; (954) 473–2955.

Everglades Holiday Park is a gateway to the largest subtropical wilderness in the continental United States. One way to get acquainted with the Everglades is by a guided forty-five-minute airboat ride. Tours run continuously from 9:00 A.M. to 5:00 P.M. daily. You'll see alligators, exotic birds, and an endless expanse of saw grass. The park is at the end of Griffin Road west of U.S. 27, about thirty minutes from Fort Lauderdale and Miami. Call (305) 434–8111.

In Fort Lauderdale when they refer to Davie, Florida, as "out west," they aren't just kidding. Davie is an authentic western town full of real live cowboys and cowgirls. If you'd like to look like they do, stop in at **Grifs Western Store,** which smells very leathery and sells all manner of boots, hats, shirts, jeans, and saddles. Even the Davie McDonald's sports a corral with salt licks, watering troughs, and hitching posts for your steed.

Come Wednesday night, folks gather in the domed ✦**Davie Rodeo Arena** for some good old-fashioned steer wrestling, calf roping, and bull riding. This is, by the way, the only weekly jackpot rodeo between Key West and Maine. The rodeo, which begins at 8:00 P.M., is on Griffin Road at Davie Road in Davie, FL 33314; (954) 384–7075.

MIAMI AREA

It's amazing what money can do. Publisher William Randolph Hearst wanted a Spanish monastery at his San Simeon castle in California, so he bought the ✦**Cloisters of the Monastery of St. Bernard de Clairvaux** and had it shipped from Europe. Only it wasn't quite as simple as it sounds. The monastery arrived in this country in 10,751 crates, but Florida customs officers wouldn't release them because they were worried about hoof-and-mouth bacteria in the packing hay. The monastery was finally reassembled, one piece of stone at a time, after Hearst's death. Built in 1141, this is the oldest building in this hemisphere. You can still see the marks early stonemasons carved in the rock. Open Sunday noon–4:00 P.M.; 10:00 A.M.–4:00 P.M. other days. Located at 16711 W. Dixie Highway in North Miami Beach, FL 33160; (305) 945–1462.

Some of the smaller hotels at the south end of Miami Beach have been getting face-lifts, and the heritage of old Miami is being preserved in the process. A square-mile area featuring the distinctive resort atmosphere of the late 1920s and 1930s is being restored. Officially known as the ◆ **Miami Beach Historic Architectural District** (fondly called the "Art Deco District"), this section contains the nation's largest collection of Art Deco structures. The buildings, totalling more than 800, are the first twentieth-century structures to be included on the National Register of Historic Places. The Art Deco District stretches from Sixth to Twenty-third streets between Alton Road and the ocean in Miami Beach. Tours are available every Saturday beginning at 10:30 A.M. from the Art Deco Welcome Center (which is open every day 10:00 A.M.–6:00 P.M.) at 1001 Ocean Drive in Miami Beach; (305) 672–2014.

Let's say you're a rock climber and find yourself in Florida. Poor choice of a place to be, you say? Not at all. You should head straight for the ◆ **Eden Roc Resort and Spa** on Miami Beach and check out the latest trend in fitness challenges—a rock climbing wall. This is the first such wall in the entire state. Here you can climb to your heart's content with other rock climbing buffs and enjoy the facilities of a first-class hotel in the process.

But the wall is just the beginning. The Eden Roc boasts the Spa of Eden, the largest oceanfront spa in the southeastern United States. This place has everything!

Its sports medicine complex comes complete with a resident exercise physiologist to conduct personal fitness and body fat evaluations. The physiologist can help determine the appropriate training level for each individual guest. An oceanfront cardiovascular theater provides the latest in computerized treadmills, cycling and stair-climbing equipment, and a sixteen-channel personal audiovisual system so you can tune into the music or TV program of your choice during your workout. A weight room featuring state-of-the-art Cybex equipment also enjoys a commanding view of the ocean.

A wide range of daily aerobics classes includes a variety of step, slide, and high and low impact choreography. Or you may prefer instruction in such innovative fitness techniques as yoga, ballet, and martial arts. Basketball courts, international squash courts, a racquetball court, an Olympic-size lap pool, an oceanside pool, and a private marina complete this extensive complex. A full complement of water sports and recreational activities offered daily from the beach includes SCUBA, kayaking, jet skiing, sailing, and parasailing.

The variety of spa services offered is staggering. Massage therapies include Swedish, deep tissue, Shiatsu, reflexology, sports massage, and aromatherapy. Body treatments range from the Algae Body Mask (detoxification and cellulite treatment), Tropical Valerian GEl Wrap (cold wrap for sunburn or relaxation), Dead Sea Mud Body and Scalp Treatment (detoxification, cleansing, and skin enrichment) to Seaweed and Salt Body Polish (restore softness to damaged skin), Sea Fango Paste (rehydrate dry skin and lymph cleansing), and Herbal Body Wrap (reduce bloating and aid circulation). Some of these treatments are offered on the glistening white sands of the resort's 600-foot sandy beach, with a grand view of the great Atlantic.

The pampering continues with Swiss showers, herbal waterfall baths, soundproof massage, and post-therapy sleep rooms. The spa's salon also offers a variety of personal grooming services including aromatic, hydrating, or lightening facials, deep-pore cleansing, waxing, herbal manicures and pedicures, acrylic and silk wrap nails, haircuts, hair coloring, permanents, and styling.

OK, OK, but where do you eat? Do you absolutely have to count calories and fat grams? The answer gives you the best of both worlds. You have a choice.

If you're a serious spa participant, you'll select the "Cuisine of Wellness" menu, which lists calories and fat grams but does not stint on flavor and presentation. Start with roasted eggplant filled with ricotta cheese and spinach, move onto a cup of tomato gazpacho, then savor stir-fry mahimahi with vegetables on soba noodles and finish it all off with blueberry mousse. The entire feast is guaranteed guilt free.

But wait a minute. You're on vacation and just want to have a good time. The Eden Roc has the answer. Jimmy Johnson's Three Rings Bar & Grill is a sports bar with TVs (and enthusiastic fans) everywhere you look. The atmosphere of this seaside eatery is very casual, and you may eat inside or outside on the expansive deck.

No wonder this is such a popular watering hole for locals as well as resort guests. The cuisine is "Floribbean," a unique blend of Florida and Caribbean cuisine (be sure to try the sweet potato fries), but the menu ought to come with a generous-portion warning. Spa goers alert! If you kick off with the super nachos, you better have at least six friends to help polish them off. The mud pie is indeed the tallest north of the South Pole, as advertised. And the double fudge brownie packs enough caloric punch to erase a week of serious fitness training.

The favorite dining spot at the Eden Roc is the Fresco Mediterranean Cafe, a fine patio-level cafe offering diverse culinary choices from the Mediterranean. Specialties from Spain, Italy, Greece, and North Africa prepared open-hearth style include a daily selection of both hot and cold tapas.

The menu poses a delicious dilemma. Should you start with pan-seared calamari, smoked beefsteak tomatoes, roasted garlic, vermouth and capers, or an array of Mediterranean vegetables with balsamic vinaigrette? Should the soup be Catalan pistou soup with roasted pheasant and white beans or cioppino spicy fish broth with mussels, shrimp, scallops, and local fish? Do you prefer grilled swordfish, arugula, and fried leek on a black fig reduction or roasted chicken rubbed with Greek spices, topped with a compote of artichokes, olives, and asparagus? You get the picture. If it's all too confusing, order a duck sausage pizza and a glass of wine, relax, and enjoy the airy ambience. Eden Roc Resort and Spa, 4525 Collins Avenue, Miami Beach, FL. (800) 327–8337 or (305) 674–5585.

The **Sonesta Beach Resort** on Key Biscayne has a terrific "Just Us Kids" program for children ages five to thirteen. Well-trained counselors supervise a wide range of fun (as well as educational) activities. Kids are taken on excursions to Metro Zoo, The Science Museum, and Seaquarium. There are also beach and pool activities, contests, games, movies, and crafts classes. Kids can participate in any part of each day's activities. The program is offered to hotel guests at no extra charge with the exception of the child's entrance fee to commercial attractions. Sonesta Beach Resort, 350 Ocean Drive, Key Biscayne, FL 33149; (305) 361–2021.

105

A distinctly Latin flavor permeates Miami, but it is most highly concentrated in its Cuban community. The Hispanic heart of the city is found in the colorful section of southwestern Miami known as ◆ **Little Havana.** This cluster of restaurants, nightclubs, cigar factories, fruit stands, and shops pulses with the energy of these lively, voluble people. Lingering over an aromatic cup of Cuban coffee and listening to Spanish may make you forget what country you're in. Little Havana is a 30-block strip on S.W. Eighth Street (known here as Calle Ocho), Miami.

◆ **Vizcaya Museum and Gardens** is a must-see. Vizcaya is James Deering's Italian Renaissance palace, one of the finest homes ever built in America. Deering, vice president of International Harvester, spent twenty years collecting priceless treasures from around the world before beginning to build a home for them in 1914. After a global search, he selected Biscayne Bay as the ideal location for his winter retreat. The seventy-room villa was finished in 1916 and the formal gardens took five years to complete, with as many as a thousand artisans working at a time. The result is a magnificent achievement featuring an extraordinary collection of furnishings and art objects as well as gardens that have been called "the finest in the Western Hemisphere." 3251 S. Miami Avenue, Miami, FL 33129. Open daily except Christmas Day 9:30 A.M.–4:30 P.M. Guided tours available. Call (305) 250–9133.

The historic pioneer home known as ◆ **The Barnacle** (1891) once belonged to one of Coconut Grove's earliest settlers, Ralph Middleton Munroe. This photographer and naval architect named the tiny village "Coconut Grove" and helped the settlement grow by encouraging his influential northern friends to visit. The resourceful Mr. Munroe first built a one-story building of wood salvaged from shipwrecks. Later, he jacked the house up on stilts and added a new first floor to make room for his growing family. Take note of Munroe's ingenious "air-conditioning" system and enjoy the lushly landscaped grounds. Guided tours are Friday, Saturday, and Sunday 9:00 and 10:30 A.M. and 1:00 and 2:30 P.M. Barnacle State Historic Site, 3485 Main Highway, Coconut Grove, FL 33133; (305) 448–9445.

In 1895 early settlers to Coconut Grove built **Plymouth Congregational Church,** which is considered South Florida's finest example of Spanish Mission architecture. Vines cover the twin belfry towers, a peacock saunters about the grounds, and the church is surrounded by native flora. No wonder this is the most sought-after wedding chapel in Miami. It is located at Main Highway and Devon Road at 3400 Devon Road, Coconut Grove, FL 33133; (305) 444-6521.

The amazing thing about **Hotel Place St. Michel,** with its vaulted ceilings, graceful arches, Spanish tiles, and antique furnishings, is that you don't need a passport to get there. This small, European-style inn has mastered the little touches that mean so much to the traveler—a basket of fruit on arrival, a newspaper delivered to your door each morning, and a hearty continental breakfast (included in the price of the room) to get you going. (Their warm, flaky croissants are immense!)

Plymouth Congregational Church

The hotel (built in 1926) has been beautifully restored, and each of the thirty rooms has its own distinct personality. Along with all the charm, it's nice to have air-conditioning, a phone, a color TV, and a friendly face at the desk eager to help. It's also wonderfully convenient to have a relaxing piano bar and elegant French restaurant (**Restaurant St. Michel**) just an elevator ride away. Breakfast is 7:00–9:30 A.M., lunch 11:30 A.M.–2:30 P.M., dinner 6:00–10:30 P.M. (11:00 P.M. on weekends). Expensive. Sunday brunch is 11:00 A.M.–2:30 P.M.

Hotel Place St. Michel and Restaurant are on the corner of Ponce de Leon Boulevard and Alcazar Avenue at 162 Alcazar Avenue, Coral Gables, FL 33134. Hotel: (305) 444–1666; restaurant: (305) 446–6572.

✦**Parrot Jungle** will delight the entire family. This lush setting with brilliantly colored tropical birds flying freely about flowering plants and trees is unique. Parrot Jungle claims to be the only natural, subtropical jungle and gardens in the United States. Besides the abundance of natural beauty, trained parrots and macaws jump rope, play poker, roller-skate, and ride bicycles in forty-minute trained bird shows every one and a half hours. A wildlife show, presented four times each day, features indigenous south Florida wildlife.

Take time to stroll leisurely along the walkways through the gardens and cactus ravine; it's hard to miss the shocking-pink flamingos at Flamingo Lake. The cafeteria serves both breakfast and lunch. Open daily 8:00 A.M.–5:00 P.M. Eleven miles south of Miami, 2½ miles off U.S. 1. Parrot Jungle, 11000 S.W. 57th Avenue, Miami, FL 33156; (305) 666–7834.

Here's a switch. At Monkey Jungle you're in the cage, and the monkeys run free. Hundreds of monkeys, gorillas, baboons, and trained chimpanzees swinging freely through a Florida rain forest obviously get a kick out of seeing you confined. Visitors enjoy performances daily in this unusual attraction that boasts the most complete collection of simians in the United States. Be sure to see the Wild Monkey Swimming Pool, the orangutan family, "King" the lowland gorilla, and the chimpanzee twins.

✦**Monkey Jungle** is also the site of one of the richest fossil deposits in southern Forida, including evidence linking the 10,000-year-old Paleo Indians to south Florida. More than 5,000 specimens have been unearthed from the limestone pit housing

Florida alligators. Open 9:30 A.M.–5:00 P.M. Take Florida Turn-pike's Homestead Extension (Highway 821) south to exit 11 (Cut-ler Ridge Boulevard/S.W. 216th Street). Once on 216th Street, go west 5 miles. Or take U.S. 1 south to 216th Street and go west 3 miles. Monkey Jungle, 14805 S.W. 216th Street, Miami, FL 33170; (305) 235–1611.

Is there such a thing as a strawberryolic? If you're one (you know who you are), better hunker down beside Burr's Straw-berry Farm because you'll never want to leave. Fresh strawberries are the main item here, but there are also tomatoes, pecans, strawberry ice, and ice-cream sundaes featuring pineapple, mango, coconut, and—surprise—strawberry. A strawberry milk-shake is a must. Burr's is at 12761 S.W. 216th Street (near Home-stead on the road to the Monkey Jungle). Open only during the winter months.

The folks at the Knaus Berry Farm make the best black bottom cake on the entire earth—not to mention outstanding cinnamon rolls, homemade breads (try the dilly bread), herb bread sticks, cookies, and, of course, berry pies, berry ice cream, and berry jellies. These folks know how to grow a strawberry.

The families who run this vegetable stand/bakery/ice-cream stand may look Amish with their long beards, black hats, bon-nets, and shawls, but they're German Baptists. They believe in peace, brotherhood, temperance, and simple living. Because they are baptized by triple immersion, they are sometimes called Dunkers, which comes from the German *tunken,* meaning to immerse.

Their stand is open 8:00 A.M.–5:30 P.M. from mid-November to late April. Knaus Berry Farm, 15980 S.W. 248th Street, Coconut Palm Drive, Homestead, FL 33031; (305) 247–0668.

Brilliantly colored tropical fish dart among the reefs, and dense forests of exotic trees, ferns, vines, shrubs, and flowers cover the low-lying land of ❖ **Biscayne National Park,** a marine park and sanctuary for marine life, water birds, boaters, snorkelers, and divers. Since most of Biscayne National Park is underwater, the only way to really tour it is by boat. This, by the way, is the largest marine sanctuary administered by the National Park Ser-vice. Certainly the tiny Convoy Point Visitor Center exhibit and few nearby picnic tables are, in themselves, hardly worth the trip. However, a park concessionaire at Convoy Point offers **glass-**

bottom-boat tours and **snorkeling trips** to the reefs, as well as island excursions for picnicking, camping, and hiking.

Biscayne has a subtropical climate that is warm and wet from May through October and mild and dry from November through April. Temperatures hover in the high 80s and low 90s in summer and range from the 60s to the low 80s in winter. High humidity and abundant sunshine are year-round features. Summer, the peak season for tropical storms and hurricanes, typically brings brief, torrential afternoon thunderstorms, but this is also the best time for diving and snorkeling because of the warmth and clarity of the water.

Convoy Point Visitor Center is 9 miles east of Homestead on North Canal Drive (S.W. 328th Street) adjacent to Homestead Bayfront Park. Access to park islands and most of the marine sanctuary is by boat only. Biscayne National Underwater Park, Inc., P.O. Box 1270, Homestead, FL 33030; (305) 230–1100.

THE EVERGLADES

There is no place like the Everglades anywhere on the planet. The Indians named it well. They called it *Pa-hay-okee,* which means grassy waters. Much of this unique wilderness consists of a shallow river percolating slowly toward the sea through a vast expanse of grass. Unlike any other river on earth, this one is 50 miles wide and a mere 6 inches deep. The water drops ever so gradually, only 15 feet over its entire 100-mile course. This is the country's largest remaining subtropical wilderness.

The river of grass seeps southward from Lake Okeechobee to the mangrove-lined rivers along the Gulf Coast through a transition zone where temperate climate blends with subtropic. The many different habitats along the way teem with life. Some plants and animals are tropical species native to the Caribbean Islands. Others are from the temperate zone.

Today the Everglades has generally come to mean all the various environments in the approximately one and a half million acres encompassed by ◆ **Everglades National Park.** Visitors reach the park by taking SR 9336 to the main park entrance, approximately 10½ miles southwest of Homestead, Florida. The park road ends at Flamingo on the southern tip of the Florida mainland, a distance of 40 miles from the entrance.

The first thing a visitor will be aware of on the drive from the main entrance are vast prairies of 10-foot-high sedge, which make up the greatest concentration of saw grass in the world. But just as vital to the intricate balance of life are mounded islands called hammocks rising above the river of grass, stands of pine and palmetto, and freshwater sloughs.

Labyrinthian mangrove forests, shallow offshore bays, and the many dollops of land known as the **Ten Thousand Islands** also are vital parts of this complex Everglades picture. Ten thousand is really just an approximation because new islands are being formed all the time, some consisting of only a few salt-tolerant mangrove trees. The area has a reputation as a fertile fishing ground, and the bird activity, especially at sunset, is impressive. This watery wilderness is easy to become lost in; it's a good idea to arrange for a guide or join a boat tour in Everglades City.

In the past, few comprehended the true value of the Glades in terms of sheer food production. This natural nursery ground supplies much of the Gulf with shrimp and the entire eastern seaboard, including New England, with fish. As a spawning ground, it is irreplaceable.

The value of the Everglades reaches far beyond a multimillion-dollar fishing industry. Few places anywhere offer greater variety of beautiful, rare, and interesting birds. About 300 species have been identified in the park, with large water birds—herons, egrets, ibises, and spoonbills—getting the greatest share of attention. The sprawling mangrove wilderness, one of the world's most unusual plant communities, is refuge for panther, bobcat, deer, raccoon, diamondback terrapin, alligator, dolphin, and manatee as well as a wide variety of fish.

Visitors to the park who expect grand scenery in the tradition of soaring mountains or great canyons will be disappointed. Getting to know the Glades is like any worthwhile relationship. It takes time. The trick to appreciating this wilderness is to be able to absorb its subtleties, and that cannot be done from behind the windows of a car. Trails range from easy walks of less than a half mile to more strenuous 14-mile hikes. There is as much life per square inch as anywhere else on earth, but this is not the kind of environment that overwhelms. This is a place that whispers.

Park officials recommend that you begin your visit with a stop at the Main Visitor Center near the main park entrance on SR 9336. There you may view a short film explaining the interrelationships of man and nature in the Everglades and pick up information that will help you understand the environment and plan your time wisely. Naturalists give hikes, talks, canoe trips, tram tours, demonstrations, and campfire programs throughout the year. Activities change daily. One day there may be a sunrise bird walk or a paddle out into Florida Bay or a slough slog cross-country or a moonlight tram tour. Ask at the visitor center for schedules. Other entrances to the park are at Shark Valley on the Tamiami Trail (U.S. 41) and at Everglades City in the northwest corner of the park.

Whether you choose to canoe through the Ten Thousand Islands, cruise the **Wilderness Waterway** by outboard, take a swamp tromp with a naturalist, or explore the various trails on your own, you will be well rewarded. You'll soon discover that the Everglades is as much an experience as it is a place. It is the incomparable pleasure of watching a great blue heron make his dainty-footed way along the shoreline, of coming upon a flock of roseate spoonbills feeding, or of listening to a dolphin take a long, deep breath. To see egrets streaming across a sinking orange sun is to glimpse but a sliver of the abundant beauty in this mysterious, ancient land.

For motel or cabin reservations for the **Flamingo Lodge** write Flamingo Lodge, Marina and Outpost, Flamingo, FL 33030. (The food at Flamingo Lodge, by the way, is very good.) Motel and cabin reservations should be made well in advance by calling (813) 695–3101. Some facilities are closed between June 1 and October 31, so be sure to call ahead.

Park campgrounds, located at Long Pine Key, Flamingo, and Chekika provide drinking water, picnic tables, grills, tent and trailer pads, and rest rooms. Flamingo has cold-water showers. Recreation vehicles are permitted, but there are no electrical, water, or sewage hookups. Campground stays are limited to fourteen days from December 1 to March 31. You may camp, without charge, at other designated sites, on beaches, or in backcountry. Access is either on foot or by boat. You must first obtain a free backcountry use permit at the park entrance station or at a ranger station.

You may explore well-marked canoe trails or chart your own course. Choose livery service or a complete camping outfit that meets the special requirements for canoeing in the Everglades. A well-marked inland water route runs from Flamingo to Everglades City. Sequentially numbered markers guide you over its 99 miles. Boats more than 18 feet long or with high cabins and windshields should not attempt the route because of narrow channels and overhanging foliage in some areas. The route requires a minimum of six hours with outboard motor or seven days by canoe. One-day round-trips are not recommended.

Campsites are available along the route. Be sure to notify a park ranger at either Flamingo or Everglades City both at the start and the end of your trip. The Flamingo marina, which can accommodate boats up to 60 feet long, rents small powered skiffs and canoes. Year-round boat tours at Flamingo travel through the mangrove wilderness and into Florida Bay.

◆ **Sightseeing boats** go into the Ten Thousand Islands region and the mangrove swamps of the northwestern Everglades. These concession-operated tours leave from the Gulf Coast Ranger Station. For information about boat tours and canoe rentals at the Gulf Coast Ranger Station, write the concessioner at Everglades National Park Boat Tours, P.O. Box 119, Everglades City, FL 33929; (941) 695–2591.

◆ **Shark Valley** lies off U.S. 41, the Tamiami Trail. Here, along the 15-mile loop road, you may see a variety of wildlife that inhabits the wide, shallow waterway, which eventually empties into Shark River. Alligators, otters, snakes, turtles, and birds, including rare wood storks and the snail kite, are native to this watery expanse. Hardwood hammocks and other tree islands dot the landscape. The loop road is used for tram rides, biking, and walking. An observation tower along the road provides a spectacular view. Reservations are recommended for tram rides during the busy winter season. For further information contact the Everglades Park Superintendent, 40001 State Road 9336, Homestead, FL 33034-6733. For tram tours call (305) 211–8455.

It's hard to believe the ◆**Miccosukee Indian Village** in the Florida Everglades is just 25 miles west of the gleaming towers of downtown Miami. Approximately 600 contemporary Miccosukees are descendants of some fifty tribespeople who escaped deportation from the United States during the Indian Wars of the last century.

Guided tours include the village of chickee huts where tribal members lived in traditional fashion. You may watch Indians wrestle alligators, take an adventurous airboat ride through the Everglades, or visit the Indian Museum, which features artifacts from various tribes.

Members of the Miccosukee tribe create and sell handmade dolls, wood carvings, beadwork, basketry, jewelry, and other crafts. The restaurant features authentic Miccosukee dishes along with standard American fare. Twenty-five miles west of Miami on U.S. 41 (Tamiami Trail), P.O. Box 440021, Miami, FL 33144. Open daily 9:00 A.M.–5:00 P.M.; (305) 223–8380.

THE KEYS

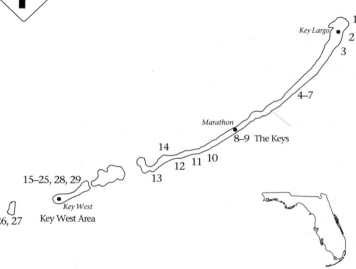

1. Overseas Highway
2. John Pennekamp Coral Reef State Park
3. *African Queen*
4. Theatre of the Sea
5. Indian Key
6. Lignumvitae Key
7. Long Key State Park
8. Hidden Harbor Turtle Hospital
9. Pigeon Key
10. Seven-Mile Bridge
11. Bahia Honda State Recreation Area
12. National Key Deer Refuge
13. Little Palm Island
14. Perky Bat Tower
15. Ernest Hemingway Home and Museum
16. Sloppy Joe's
17. Audubon House
18. Mel Fisher Maritime Heritage Society Museum
19. Wrecker's Museum
20. Duval Street
21. Old Island Days
22. Conch Tour Train
23. East Martello Tower Museum
24. Key West Lighthouse Museum
25. Fort Zachary Taylor
26. Fort Jefferson
27. Dry Tortugas
28. Southernmost Point
29. Mallory Docks

THE KEYS

The Keys gleam like gems set in a sea that dazzles from transparent turquoise and milky emerald to deep sapphire. Strung on a ribbon of concrete and steel better known as the ◆ **Overseas Highway,** this archipelago curves 100 miles from Biscayne Bay to Key West. Nearly 70 miles west of the highway's end in Key West are a few leftover jewels, which Ponce de Leon christened the Tortugas (Spanish for turtles).

These frost-free islands, warmed by the Gulf Stream in winter and cooled by the trade winds in summer, appear to be an uncomplicated antidote for the winter weary. Nothing in their swaying palms or glistening sandy beaches offers the slightest hint of a tempestuous past.

Yet early history of the Keys is peppered with both drama and tragedy. Ponce de Leon, who claimed Florida for Spain in 1513, charted the Keys and named them Los Martires (The Martyrs), because from a distance they looked like men who were suffering. The name proved to be prophetic. Spanish ships, laden with gold and treasures from Central America, were routinely plundered as they passed the islands. Such famous pirates as Black Caesar, Blackbeard, and Lafitte found the Keys' many inlets and coves ideal for concealing their ships and stashing their booty.

By the turn of the century, the Keys were more than ready for tycoon Henry Flagler's incredible scheme to link them to the mainland by rail. His idea was to extend his famous Florida East Coast Railroad across 100 miles of water and twenty-nine islands. As one of the founders of Standard Oil, Flagler had plenty of wealth to devote to this grand project popularly known as Flagler's Folly. At age seventy-five, having spent a lifetime responding to improbable challenges, he could afford to ignore those who said it couldn't be done. Besides, it didn't seem like such a big deal. "All you have to do," he said, "is to build one concrete arch, and then another, and pretty soon you will find yourself in Key West."

Unfortunately, the railroad turned out to be an economic failure. To make matters worse, a horrendous hurricane tore through the Keys in 1935, destroying embankments and even sweeping a train into the sea. After nearly two and one-half years of relative isolation, the impoverished people of the Keys were delighted when the state of Florida built the 128-mile Overseas Highway. The highway, a continuation of U.S. 1, is an incredible engineering feat consisting of 113 miles of roadway and forty-three bridges.

Residents of the Keys, buoyed by their new accessibility, placed their hope for the future in tourism, a hope that has become reality. More than a million tourists each year seek out the Keys' subtropical climate and easygoing island lifestyle. They are usually in quest of an off-the-beaten-path experience, and they are rarely disappointed with what they find. You can traverse the highway in less than three hours; but then, you can also see the Mona Lisa in less than a minute. The point is to take your time and enjoy. There are lots of things to see and do, but you will need to slow down to fully absorb and appreciate the natural beauty that surrounds you.

The Upper Keys, those nearest the mainland, stretch from Key Largo through Long Key. Key Largo is the base for the nation's first underwater park. ◆**John Pennekamp Coral Reef State Park,** 21 miles long and approximately 4 miles wide, protects forty species of coral and 650 species of fish on the only living reef along the Atlantic Coast. The reef, which was severely damaged by commercial souvenir hunters in the 1930s and 1940s, has recovered under the park's protection. These spectacular coral gardens were saved by a conservation movement spearheaded by John Pennekamp, an associate editor of the *Miami Herald,* whose stories fired up public interest in this national treasure.

Dive shops abound in Key Largo as do scuba diving courses culminating in certification. Skin divers, snorkelers, and passengers on glass-bottom boats revel in the park's clearwater views to 60 feet, which include colorful coral formations, exotic fish, turtles, and old sailing wrecks. *Christ of the Deep,* a replica of Guido Galletti's *Christ of the Abyss* in the Mediterranean Sea, highlights one of the reef's natural underwater valleys.

A glass-bottom boat leaves three times daily (9:15 A.M., 12:15 P.M., and 3:00 P.M.) for a guided tour of **Molasses Reef.** You'll see high coral ridges, tunnels, and a variety of formations including elkhorn, staghorn, star, and brain coral without ever getting wet. Certified scuba divers may board a boat that leaves daily at 9:30 A.M. and 1:30 P.M. for trips to Molasses Reef, French Reef, or Benwood Wreck (depending on conditions). Snorkelers take advantage of a convenient dive platform on *El Capitan,* which leaves three times daily on two-and-a-half-hour reef trips. Usually the excursion heads for Grecian Rocks where you'll see colorful angelfish, parrotfish, and some harmless nurse sharks. For boat tour information call (305) 451–1621.

John Pennekamp Park also has canoe and windsurfer rentals as well as beaches and nature trails. The campsites are much in demand, so be sure to make reservations well ahead or get there early. John Pennekamp Coral Reef State Park, P.O. Box 487, Key Largo, FL 33037; (305) 451–1202.

At the **Key Largo Holiday Inn** you may see the ❖*African Queen,* an old river freighter that Humphrey Bogart and Katharine Hepburn made famous in the 1951 film classic. The remodeled inn now has a Casa Blanca Lounge and Greenstreet's Restaurant.

❖ **Theatre of the Sea** in Islamorada (Spanish for Purple Isle) is the second-oldest marine-life park in the world. A ninety-minute tour includes a look at an extensive shark and ray collection and a dolphin show in a natural coral grotto. Who knows? This may be your only chance to be kissed by an affectionate sea lion or touch a shark (and come away with all your fingers intact). For information and reservations on the "Swim with a Dolphin" program, call (305) 664–2431. Open 9:30 A.M.–4:00 P.M. daily. Theatre of the Sea is on U.S. 1, P.O. Box 407, Islamorada, FL 33036; (305) 664–2431.

From Indian Key Fill on U.S. 1, you can take boat tours of both Lignumvitae Key and Indian Key. Boat tours leave for ❖**Indian Key** State Historic Site at 10:00 A.M. and 2:00 P.M. and for ❖**Lignumvitae Key** State Botanical Site at 9:00 A.M. and 1:00 P.M. Closed Tuesday and Wednesday. Lignumvitae was named for a type of hardwood tree with healing properties found growing here, and tours of the State Botanical Site reveal many other unusual plants. You'll be fascinated to learn how early Keys residents adapted the fruits, barks, and leaves of the forest to meet their needs. Rangers say this nature preserve "is the last place that truly represents the Keys as they were."

A once-thriving settlement at Indian Key (a state historic site) was completely destroyed during the Seminole Indian raid in 1840. The tropical foliage here is amazing. Only at the top of the observation tower are you eye level with the tops of towering century plants. A marvelous time to visit is May when tiny white butterflies are migrating from South America. ❖ **Long Key State Park** is noted for great fishing, swimming, snorkeling, boating, and camping. For information about the park contact Park Manager, P.O. Box 776, Long Key, FL 33001; (305) 664-4815.

The Middle and Lower Keys (from Long Key on to Key West) differ geologically from the Upper Keys, which are the boney skeletons of an ancient coral reef. While all the islands have as a base a thick blanket of limestone, those farther from the mainland are topped with a layer of Miami oolite, egg-shaped particles cemented into rock by the millennium.

Each island seems to have a distinct identity, but most activities still center on Key favorites—beachcombing, sun basking, and fishing from bridge, beach, and boat. From Marathon to Key West, spearfishing is permitted 1 mile offshore. Marathon is the starting point for the famous ❖ **Seven-Mile Bridge,** the country's longest continuous bridge. Its 65-foot crest is the highest point in the Keys.

Once it was a strip joint; in fact, it was the only topless dancer bar on Marathon Key. Now Fanny's Bar is—ta da—the nation's only turtle hospital. Some would call this progress.

Unfortunately, ❖ **Hidden Harbor Turtle Hospital** came into being to solve a growing problem—turtles afflicted with multiple tumors. These tumors are symptoms of a debilitating disease known as Fibro-Papilloma that is now thought to have viral origins. This rapidly spreading epidemic may be affecting as much as 90 percent of the local turtle population and has shown up as far away as Barbados and Hawaii.

Back in 1986 Tina Brown, charter boat captain, and her partner Richie Moretti, one-time auto mechanic, purchased the Hidden Harbor Motel and converted their saltwater pool for the display of marine life. Soon local anglers began bringing in turtles suffering from grotesque tumors, and it became clear surgery was needed to save their lives.

Brown and Moretti bartered free fishing and diving trips for the services of a vet until they were able to get a vet on staff who would perform surgery in exchange for a room. They fund their hospital (which needs roughly $100,000 yearly) from proceeds of the Hidden Harbor Motel and give countless hours to the care of their reptilian friends.

They also give educational programs to local school children and presentations on turtles to the local museum. Currently Brown and Moretti are working with the University of Florida in hopes of finding a cure for a disease that is decimating an already endangered species.

The turtle hospital does not have regular visiting hours for the public, but it is possible to arrange a tour if you call in advance. You will be amazed at the modern medical offices—including an X-ray room, necropsy lab, and operating room—and saddened by the sight of so many sick turtles in the saltwater pool behind the hospital. Ask for Tina Brown at the Hidden Harbor Turtle Hospital, 2390 Overseas Highway, Marathon, FL 33050; (305) 743–5376.

If it's late in the day and you need a place to sleep, why not consider a floating houseboat at dockside or a lighthouse apartment. **Faro Blanco Marine Resort** offers both as well as an assortment of cottages and condos, four restaurants, a full service marina, Olympic-size swimming pool, charter fishing, tours, and dive lessons. The resort has facilities on both Atlantic and Gulf waters.

Faro Blanco is in Marathon, 110 miles southwest of the Florida mainland, two and one-half hours from Miami by car, an hour from Key Largo, or an hour from Key West. The resort is located at mile marker 48. Faro Blanco Marine Resort, 1996 Overseas Highway, Marathon, FL 33050; (800) 759–3276 or (305) 743–9018.

It's easy to whiz right by ◆**Pigeon Key** as you drive across Seven-Mile Bridge. You might look down, see a cluster of old buildings on a tiny palm-sheltered island, and wonder what it's all about. Of course you'd like to take a closer look. Those with a yen to get off the fast track for a little while will be well rewarded by a brief sojourn to Pigeon Key.

This four-acre island, connected to the mainland by a bridge originally built by Henry Flagler for his famous Florida East Coast Railway, has a rich and colorful history. Today its future seems equally promising. Pigeon Key, virtually in the shadow of the Overseas Highway, is a certified Historic District listed on the National Register of Historic Places. From 1908 to 1935, this island served as a construction and maintenance camp for the railroad; The Pigeon Key Foundation has carefully restored seven buildings from this era.

Since the railroad days, Pigeon Key has been a center for the Road and Toll District, a site for the U.S. Navy, a fishing camp, and a research center for the University of Miami.

The potential for this idyllic island is limitless; it is on its way, gradually but certainly, to becoming a world-class center for environmental education, historical exhibits, and research.

Be sure to sign up for a tour and take the shuttle out to the island. You'll enjoy the ride. The shuttle is an attractive railroad car, originally part of the historic Florida East Coast Railway that leaves from the Pigeon Key Visitor's Center on Knight's Key. This way you'll hear stories of the early railroad as you pass slowly over the Old Seven-Mile Bridge.

Shuttle to Pigeon Key

Once you reach the island, you'll learn about the heritage of the Florida Keys, the natural environment, and various disastrous hurricanes. Your guide will make memories of one-time residents come alive. And, yes, the island has a ghost, or at least a fairly juicy ghost story.

Be sure to see the historical and cultural exhibits, including "Florinda," a Cuban refugee vessel that carried twenty-four people to freedom, and learn all about the old buildings. You'll see the Section Gang's Quarters (1909), a one-time dorm for railway workers (now the Education Center for the Pigeon Key Foundation); the Bridge Tender's House (1909); the Bridge Foreman's House (1916); Negro Quarters (1909); Honeymoon Cottage (1950); and others. Don't miss the 1930 *Home Movie* of a trip on the Florida East Coast Railway from Key West to Miami shown in the Education Center.

Pigeon Key is a delightful spot for a picnic (you're welcome to use the picnic tables), or you may want to just sit beside the sea and watch the colors shift from aquamarine to cobalt. Artists and photographers return time after time to capture the island's picturesque landscapes and seascapes.

The island's proximity to the Gulf Stream, Florida Bay, coral reefs, sea grass beds, and an abundant variety of marine life makes it an ideal setting for marine research. Mote Marine Laboratory plans to use the island's resources to study such vital concerns as water quality and the biological integrity of tropical marine ecosystems. Mote's Center for Shark Research will continue its study of sharks as an ecologically and economically valuable marine resource.

Approximately 45 miles from Key West, 100 miles southwest of Miami, and 2⅗ miles due west of Marathon, Pigeon Key is connected to the mainland by the Old Seven-Mile Bridge.

Sounds interesting but how do you get to Pigeon Key? Walkers, joggers, cyclists, and skaters are welcome to go out to Pigeon Key via the Old Seven-Mile Bridge at any time during regular hours (9:00 A.M.–5:00 P.M. Tuesday through Sunday) for a small admission fee. Access to the island is at mile marker 48 at the west end of Marathon.

One thing you can't do is drive your car to Pigeon Key as regulations prohibit private cars on the old bridge. You may, however, leave your car in the parking lot at the east end of the Old Seven-Mile Bridge.

The best way to experience this historic island is to begin and end your trip at the Pigeon Key Visitor's Center on the Atlantic side of Knight's Key. Even if you don't have time to meander about Pigeon Key, take a moment to browse the visitor's center's intriguing selection of environmental and historical books and gifts.

The shuttle service to Pigeon Key leaves Knight's Key on the hour from 10:00 A.M. to 4:00 P.M. Visitors are welcome to stay as long as they wish and to return on any shuttle. The last shuttle returns to the visitor's center at 5:00 P.M. Why not make a day of it? Pigeon Key Foundation, P.O. Box 500130, Marathon, FL 33050; (305) 289–0025.

Prettiest beach in the Florida Keys? Consider ❖ **Bahia Honda State Recreation Area** just south of Marathon's Seven-Mile Bridge. The idyllic, palm-shaded beach at Bahia Honda (Spanish for deep bay) resembles a tropical island in the South Pacific. Pines, palms, and mangroves frame ocean views that shift from turquoise and violet to milky emerald and navy blue. The water temperature ranges from the low to mid-80s, and refreshing Caribbean trade winds keep this sunbaked subtropical island comfortable year-round.

This southernmost state park is the perfect place to while away the hours beachcombing, swimming, snorkeling, fishing, exploring, and bird-watching. Be sure to stroll the nature trail to see some of the unusual botanical growth (satinwood trees, spiny catesbaeas, and dwarf morning glories) on this unique spit of land as well as the many beautiful and rare birds (white-crowned pigeon, great white heron, roseate spoonbill, reddish egret, osprey, brown pelican, and least terns) that pass through here.

For a glorious view climb the old **Bahia Honda Bridge,** which includes the original Flagler train trestle and the abandoned narrow span where more than one RV lost an outside mirror in a highway squeeze play. Many of the old bridges in the Upper and Lower Keys, including this one, offer anglers spots to dangle their hooks for mackerel, bluefish, tarpon, snook, grouper, and jewfish. According to a park ranger, tarpon fishing in Bahia Honda rates among the best in the country.

Two campgrounds—one fairly open near the marina and west

123

swimming area, the other shady and more secluded—tempt RVers and tent campers to linger. Typical of Florida state parks, this one is clean and well-maintained. Reservations are suggested, especially around holidays. Half the campsites are reserved for those who call ahead (reservations taken up to sixty days in advance), and half are booked on a first-come, first-served basis. There are six cabins, which may be reserved up to a year in advance. Bahia Honda State Recreation Area, 35850 Overseas Highway, Big Pine Key, FL 33043; (305) 872–2353.

Dainty Key deer wander through the slash pines and mangrove swamps on Big Pine and a few surrounding keys. This fragile sub-species, thought to have been stranded when the Wisconsin Glacier melted, is the smallest of all whitetail deer. From 26 to 32 inches in height, the deer average 38 inches in length and weigh between 30 and 110 pounds. By 1954 hunting and destruction of habitat had reduced the population of deer to fifty. The estab-lishment of a ◈**National Key Deer Refuge** protected the herd, which has stabilized at about 300. These deer, the size of a large dog, are still threatened with extinction, primarily because of loss of habitat and ill-advised feeding by residents and visitors. Feeding can cause the deer to congregate and bring them in con-tact with such death traps as cars, canals, fences, and dogs. It is now against the law to feed the deer.

National Key Deer Refuge is north of U.S. 1 on Key Deer Boule-vard (SR 940). The refuge headquarters is in the Winn Dixie shop-ping center on Key Deer Boulevard, Big Pine Key. Best times to see deer are early morning, late afternoon, and early evening. **Blue Hole,** a rock quarry with a mean old alligator guarding a sign that says PLEASE DON'T FEED THE ALLIGATORS, is nearby. For infor-mation contact the Refuge Manager at (305) 872–2239.

If you don't feel romantic on ◈**Little Palm Island,** you'd better check your pulse. This is the place romantics dream about, a secluded South Seas kind of island abloom with lush tropical foliage including a dense grove of soaring Jamaican coconut palms. And get this—you don't have to jet the vast reaches of the South Pacific to find this idyllic retreat. It's just 3 miles offshore in the heart of the Florida Keys.

Once upon a time, this five-acre island served as a fishing camp and private getaway for Presidents Roosevelt, Truman, Kennedy, and Nixon plus a string of other dignitaries and celebrities. Since

1988 it's been a luxury resort for those seeking the ultimate escape from reality.

As you approach the island, you'll catch a glimpse of thatched roofs peaking from beneath luxuriant greenery. These roofs belong to fourteen stilted villas scattered throughout the island. Each private abode comes with a secluded, wraparound sundeck, an enticing rope hammock strung between gracefully curved palm trees, and an ocean view.

Inside you'll find a living room, an expansive bedroom with king-sized bed draped in gauzy, for-effect-only mosquito netting, and a sitting area. The dressing area and bathroom, complete with whirlpool bath, open directly to a bamboo-fenced, totally private outdoor shower. Go ahead and pinch yourself. Try to remember this is not Fiji; this is Florida.

Every modern comfort is at your disposal, from a minibar to a wet bar with plenty of coffee and tea. However, you will not find the spirit-jarring intrusions of television, telephones, and alarm clocks. They are banned from the island. After all, this is supposed to be a romantic hideaway.

Tropical islands usually unveil their flaws on closer inspection. What Little Palm Island reveals is a heated lagoonlike freshwater pool fringed by palms, a waterfall, flowering shrubs, birds, and a sugar-white sandy beach.

You now have a tough decision. Do you simply relax and enjoy the ambience, or do you take advantage of the resort's many activities? Windsurfers, kayaks, canoes, sailboats, fishing equipment, and snorkeling gear are complimentary. You may want to perk up your appetite with a workout in the exercise room near the Gift Boutique.

Perhaps you'd rather go scuba diving, snorkeling, or try your hand at deep-sea fishing. Several offshore and mainland excursions are offered, and guided nature tours by canoe or sailboat are popular. Divers will definitely want to join an excursion to nearby Looe Key to explore the wonders of the last living coral reef in North America.

If your idea of a vacation is simply to relax and be pampered, you'll want to indulge yourself with a spa treatment including a relaxing massage, a facial, and a manicure or pedicure.

Little Palm Island is a delightful spot to enjoy wildlife. Great white herons, little green herons, night herons, frigate birds, white ibis, brown pelicans, osprey, skimmers, egrets, sandpipers, roseate spoonbills, manatees, dolphin, Key deer, and loggerhead turtles are common sights in the four separate nature preserves near the island and on the surrounding ocean flats.

The island is on the flyway for birds making their spring migratory trip north from the Caribbean basin and Central and South America. Bird migration peaks in early May and continues throughout the month. More than 100 migratory species include blackpoll warblers, palm warblers, falcons, kestrels, orioles, tanagers, bobolinks, cuckoos, ovenbirds, and black-bellied plovers.

A pair of wild parrots, named "Harry" and "Bess" in honor of the Trumans who once visited the island, occasionally fly in for breakfast and dinner. The staff welcomes them even though they fly in the face of a firm resort policy mandating reservations for those not registered.

The resort dock is a favorite hangout for tarpon, bonefish, angelfish, snapper, lookdown fish, and snook. Sometimes in the evenings hundreds of great tarpon roll around in the deep water at the end of the dock.

You'll notice a sign by the outdoor dining room indicating it is off limits to Key Deer. These deer know a good menu when they catch wind of it. These diminutive mammals often swim over to Little Palm from a neighboring island to see what's going on. If they don't show up for dinner, you can commandeer a canoe the next day and paddle to nearby Big Munson Island, home to a herd of about thirty endangered deer.

One thing all resort guests seem to enjoy is eating. The island's gourmet cuisine combines classic and nouvelle French with American-style cooking, including both Caribbean and Oriental embellishments. You might tease the appetite with smoked-salmon parfait with Belgian endive and green apple, or a wild mushroom and conch lasagna. It's hard to beat an entree of locally caught stone crab claws, but the chef's signature rack of lamb, seared with mustard and crusted with herbs and breadcrumbs, gives it a good run for its money. If you're in the mood for a totally decadent dessert, select the coconut cream-filled chocolate ravioli with praline sauce. Oh my.

You may order breakfast served in your room or on your private deck. For lunch and dinner you may dine in the airy dining room, outdoors on a spacious terrace, or a few steps down on the resort's pristine sandy beach. The Tropical Sunday Brunch buffet is an island tradition, and the chef creates a different seven-course feast each Thursday. You don't need to be a resort guest to take advantage of the superb cuisine on any day, but you do need a reservation. The public may make dining reservations by calling (305) 872–2551.

Little Palm Resort is at the western end of the Newfound Harbor Keys, where the Gulf of Mexico meets the Straits of Florida. The island is a fifteen-minute launch ride from its Shore Station on Little Torch Key. Little Torch Key is on Overseas Highway U.S. 1 at mile marker 28.5, approximately 28 miles east of Key West International Airport, 22 miles south of Marathon Airport, and 120 miles southwest of Miami International Airport.

Transfer and van service to the Little Torch Key Shore Station is available from both Key West and Marathon Airports. Limousine service can be arranged from Key West, Marathon, and Miami International Airports. Seaplane and helicopter service is available from Miami. Advance notice is required for all these services. Little Palm Island, 28500 Overseas Highway, Little Torch Key, FL; 33042; (305) 872–2524 or (800) 3–GET–LOST.

Now here's a batty idea—a highrise for bats. This weather-beaten, 35-foot wooden tower was built to solve a problem. You see, Righter Clyde Perky wanted tourists to enjoy his guest cottages, restaurant, and marina, but they were turned off by hordes of dive-bombing mosquitoes. Perky knew bats had a ravenous appetite for mosquitoes, so he built them the most comfortable lodging he could think of and decorated it with sex-scented bat droppings imported from Texas. Unfortunately, the bats never got wind of the project (although the neighbors certainly did), and the tower remains uninhabited. Modern spraying techniques have largely done away with the mosquito problem, and who can say the tower isn't a success in its own right—after all, it has survived several hurricanes and is listed on the National Register of Historic Places. The ◆ **Perky Bat Tower** is near mile marker 17 on the Gulf side of U.S. 1 on Sugarloaf Key.

KEY WEST AREA

At the end of the Overseas Highway where the Atlantic meets the Gulf of Mexico is Key West, the southernmost city in the

Perky Bat Tower

Continental United States. Here the Calusa Indians made a final stand against invading tribes from the north. The Spanish, who came upon the grisly remains of the battle, named it *Cayo Hueso,* which translates to the "island of bones." Eventually this was anglicized into Key West.

Unruffled by the crosscurrents of its cultural heritage, this exotic community has long been a mecca for writers, artists, and other well-knowns. The claim is that Key West is not really a place, but an attitude. The community's freewheeling spirit once led it to secede from the Union, establish the Conch Republic, and demand foreign aid from the United States government! On this 5-by-3-mile island Tennessee Williams spent the final years of his life, Harry Truman had his **Little White House,** and John James Audubon painted tropical birds.

Stop in to visit the six-toed cats (direct descendants of those loved by "Papa" Hemingway) at the ❖ **Ernest Hemingway Home and Museum.** Hemingway bought this Spanish Colonial–style house in 1931 and wrote a number of novels here. You'll see memorabilia, original furnishings, and exotic trees and plants from around the world. Open daily 9:00 A.M.–5:00 P.M., 907 Whitehead Street, Key West, FL 33040; (305) 294–1575.

More Hemingway memorabilia is on tap at ❖ **Sloppy Joe's,** Papa's favorite bar at 201 Duval Street, Key West, FL 33040.

The ❖ **Audubon House** contains many of John J. Audubon's original engravings as well as a video about his life. Authentically restored with eighteenth- and nineteenth-century furnishings, this early-nineteenth-century house is now a public museum. Once you've seen the incredible bird life on the Keys, it's not hard to understand why this famed naturalist-artist spent so much time here. The Audubon House is at 205 Whitehead Street at Green Street, Key West, FL 33040. Open daily 9:30 A.M.–5:00 P.M.; (305) 294–2116.

The ❖ **Mel Fisher Maritime Heritage Society Museum** has treasures recovered from Spanish galleons that have been slumbering on the ocean floor for centuries. Along with more than 150 pounds of gold are silver bullion, emeralds, diamonds, copper, brass cannons, rare antiques, and a wonderful collection of historic artifacts. All told, the treasure, worth more than $40 million, is one of the largest displays of its type anywhere.

Feast your eyes on gold doubloons and discs, more than fifty gold bars, and thirty-five gold chains—including one measuring 12 feet and weighing more than six pounds. The prize piece from the salvaged collection is a gold poison cup featuring a bezoar stone that changes color when it comes in contact with a toxic substance. You just can't be too careful! Mel Fisher's Gold Exhibit is at 200 Greene Street, Key West, FL 33040. Open 9:30 A.M.–5:00 P.M. daily; (305) 294–2633.

Once shipwrecks were the area's economic mainstay. Settlers from the mainland, the Bahamas, and Europe flocked to the Keys to partake in the rich harvest of the sea. In 1825 Congress legislated that all salvage taken from wrecks in United States waters must be taken to a United States port for arbitration. Key West, as the islands' first permanent settlement, became the center for the auction of cargoes and repair of ships. By the 1830s wrecking had made Key West the wealthiest city, per capita, in the entire United States of America. The long dreary years of economic draught that followed were not endured in vain. Had the town enjoyed a history of uninterrupted prosperity rather than prolonged recession, its architectural treasure trove might have been leveled to make way for more modern buildings.

The ✦ **Wrecker's Museum** in the Oldest House in Key West is actually two houses, typical of 1830s "conch" construction. Browse the displays on the wrecking industry that once made Key West such a wealthy community. Don't miss the elegantly furnished dollhouse, the old kitchen house, and large garden. Guided tours 10:00 A.M.–4:00 P.M. Maintained by the Old Island Restoration Foundation, 322 Duval Street, Key West, FL 33040; (305) 294–9502.

A massive restoration effort, centered on ✦ **Duval Street,** is currently saving classic buildings that infuse the city with its Old World air. The architecture is a melange of Bahamian, Spanish, New England, and Southern styles. The Oldest House (circa 1829) in Key West is typical of small residences of that time. Many old homes were built in the 1850s by master ship carpenters who insisted on the best materials and used wooden pegs instead of nails. These handsome homes with wide verandas and gingerbread trim suggest a slower, more gracious era. Some of the most attractive, known as "conch" houses, were built in sections in the Bahamas and shipped over on schooners.

If you can possibly schedule your visit to coincide with

❖**Old Island Days,** which begin in January and end in March, do so. The residents of this small island community wear bright red and white to mark the festivities as the entire island celebrates its heritage with house and garden tours, food fests, plays, flower shows, sidewalk art festivals, and even a conch-shell blowing contest. For information contact Florida Keys and Key West Visitors Bureau, 402 Wall Street, Key West, FL 33040; or call (305) 294–1241 (arts and crafts show information) or (305) 294–9501 (house tours).

Natives of Key West are called *Conchs* (pronounced "konks") for the mollusk that thrives in local waters. This favorite local delicacy appears in chowders, fritters, conch salad, and as conch steak. Don't leave the islands without sampling stone crab, Florida lobster, shrimp, and fresh-off-the-boat swordfish, yellow-tail, and red snapper. This is the perfect place to indulge in traditional Cuban dishes. Be sure to try a bowl of black bean soup and some bollos (pronounced "bowyows"), hush puppies made with mashed, shelled black-eyed peas instead of cornmeal. For dessert, Key lime pie, made from the piquant Key limes that flourish here, wins hands down.

Tourists who take the ❖**Conch Tour Train,** an open-air tram, get a good look at the restoration area as well as the island's major points of interest. This one-and-a-half-hour tour promises "sixty of the most unusual historical sites you've ever seen." Boarding locations are Mallory Square and Roosevelt Avenue. Tours leave approximately every half hour 9:00 A.M.–4:30 P.M. daily. Contact Conch Tour Train at No. 1 Key Lime Square, Key West, FL 33040; (305) 294–5161.

History buffs will want to visit the ❖**East Martello Tower Museum,** part of the nineteenth-century effort to fortify the country's southern boundary. Ground was broken for East Martello Tower in 1861, but the fort was never involved in a battle. A large collection of artifacts from the Keys (including implements used in cigar making and sponge diving) is housed in the fort's long series of casements, and two permanent art collections are on display. East Martello Gallery and Museum is adjacent to the airport at 3500 S. Roosevelt Boulevard, Key West, FL 33040. Open 9:30 A.M.–5:30 P.M. daily; (305) 296–3913.

You'll get a commanding view from the newly restored 110-foot tower of the lighthouse in the ❖**Key West Lighthouse**

Museum. Built in 1847, the museum pays tribute to the unique military history of the Florida Keys and contains many military artifacts. Open daily 9:30 A.M.–4:30 P.M. Key West Lighthouse Museum, 938 Whitehead Street, Key West, FL 33040; (305) 294–0012.

Key West's newest state park, dedicated on July 4, 1985, is ◆**Fort Zachary Taylor.** This pre–Civil War fortress is a reminder of a time when Union troops occupied Key West during the Civil War. To uncover Fort Taylor's mysteries, Howard England worked alone for nine years with bucket and shovel to uncover the country's largest known collection of Civil War cannons. He assembled a small museum with artifacts, photographs, and a model of the original fort. The park, with one of the finest natural beaches on the island, is an ideal spot to swim and picnic. Open 8:00 A.M. to sunset every day. Fort Taylor, P.O. Box 289, Key West, FL 33041. For information call (305) 292–6713.

At Key West arrangements can be made to fly 68 miles west to ◆**Fort Jefferson** and **Dry Tortugas National Park.** The low-flying seaplane passes over shifting sandbars, clearly identifiable sharks, and an old Spanish wreck that has coughed up millions of dollars worth of treasure. Passengers look down on the Marquesas, a ring of islands considered by some to be the only atoll in the Atlantic Ocean.

The Tortugas were considered of great strategic importance to the United States. Because the U.S. War Department believed the nation that occupied these islands could protect navigation in the Gulf, it decided to fortify them. Construction began on Fort Jefferson in 1846. Complete with 50-foot-high walls and a water-filled moat, the hexagonal fort covered most of sixteen-acre Garden Key. It was to be the strongest link in the chain of coastal forts that reached from Maine to Texas during the first half of the 1800s.

Federal troops occupied Fort Jefferson throughout the Civil War but saw little action. Although work continued on the fort for thirty years, it was never completed primarily because the new rifled cannon introduced during the war had already made it obsolete. Used as a military stronghold for captured deserters during the Civil War, Fort Jefferson continued as a prison for almost ten years after the fighting had ceased.

The fort's most famous prisoner was Dr. Samuel Mudd, the physician who set John Wilkes Booth's broken leg after Booth assassinated Abraham Lincoln. Brought here in 1865 and sentenced to a lifetime of hard labor, he earned an early pardon by tirelessly tending to the victims of a yellow fever epidemic that swept through the fort. Be sure to see the orientation slide program before taking the self-guiding tour.

Snorkeling is especially good off the moat walls of Fort Jefferson. Coral formations and brilliant tropical fish provide fine opportunities for underwater photography. Saltwater fishing is good most of the year and no fishing license is required.

Fort Jefferson Visitor Center is open 8:00 A.M.–5:00 P.M. Public transportation to the fort is available from Key West by seaplane or boat. Those who want to go by private boat may purchase nautical charts at marinas and boating supply outlets in Key West. Boaters should be aware of the possibility of extremely rough seas. The Tortugas are isolated, and you must provide for yourself. No housing, water, meals, or supplies are available. Camping is permitted in the grassed picnic area. For more information write the Superintendent, Box 6208, Key West, FL 33040; (305) 242–7700. For information on charter boats and flights, contact the Greater Key West Chamber of Commerce, 402 Wall Street, Old Mallory Square, Key West, FL 33040; (305) 294–2587 or (800) 878–FISH.

Frigate birds with 7-foot wingspans soar above the cerulean waters surrounding the ◆**Dry Tortugas.** Sooty terns, which have turned Bush Key into a rookery, lay their eggs in shallow depressions on its warm sandy beaches. The Tortugas also host noddy terns, brown and blue-faced boobies, and a variety of passing songbirds en route from Cuba and South America. During the nesting season from March to October, Bush Key is reserved for birds only. All keys, other than Garden Key and Loggerhead Key, are closed during the turtle season from May through the end of September.

Visitors should not leave Key West without seeing the ◆**Southernmost Point** in the continental United States. (The Big Island of Hawaii claims the honor for the nation.) Chinese immigrant Jim Kee began selling shells here in the late 1930s, and his descendants still cater to tourists' yen for souvenirs.

Some of Key West's appeal is its temperature, which varies only twelve degrees and averages a balmy 77°, and some is its luxuriant palms, hibiscus, oleander, bougainvillaea, and fragrant frangipani blooms. But the city's greatest charm is that it is a true original. Few other communities have the good sense to celebrate such a daily marvel as the sunset. The crowd starts to gather at ❖ **Mallory Docks** about half an hour before the main event. The Cookie Lady arrives on her bicycle and does a bustling business selling warm brownies and cookies. Locals show off their parrots and pet iguanas. Some juggle, dance, sing, or swallow flaming swords. All the entertainment is free (although the entertainers do pass a hat). After the sun's final farewell, everyone heartily applauds the performance.

For those who have purposely strayed far from the beaten path, it is an entirely appropriate celebration—a fine way to end a day or, for that matter, a book.

INDEX

Botanical Garden, 46
Bristol, 37
Brooksville, 67
Buffalo Trading Co., 50
Bulow Plantation Ruins
    Historic Site, 1, 12
Bunnell, 12
Burr's Strawberry Farm, 109
Burt Reynolds' Ranch, 96
Bush Key, 133
Bushnell, 66
Butler Mill Trail, 38
By Word of Mouth
    Restaurant, 100

C
Cabbage Key, 73, 86
Ca'd'Zan, 74
Cafe Alcazar, 1, 10
Caladesi Island, 41, 62
Calle Ocho, 106
Caloosahatchee River, 87
Canaveral National Seashore,
    41, 45
Canoe Outpost, 73, 84
Cape Haze, 80
Cap's Place, 93, 98
Captain Anderson's Marina,
    25
Captiva Island, 85
Carillon Tower, 18, 54
Carrabelle, 23
Castillo de San Marcos, 1, 9
Castillo de San Marcos Nat'l
    Monument, 1, 9
Casual Clam Cafe, 82
Cattle auction, 51
Cedar Key, 17, 19
Cedar Key Chamber of
    Commerce, 20

Cedar Key Hist. Society
    Museum, 20
Cedar Key Wildlife Refuge, 20
Cedar Key State Museum, 20
Central Atlantic Coast, 42
Central Florida, 41
Central Heartland, 52
Centre Street Fernandina, 1, 2
Chalet Suzanne Inn and
    Restaurant, 53
Chattahoochee River, 37
Chautauqua Assembly Build-
    ing, 34
Cheyenne Saloon & Opera
    House, 50
Chipley, 36
Choctowhatchee Bay, 26
Christ of the Deep, 117
Christmas Concerts, 18
Church Street Station, 41, 50
Circus Galleries, 73, 74
Cloister, The, 98
Cloisters of the Monastery of
    St. Bernard de Clairvaux,
    93, 102
Coastal Panhandle, 20
Coconut Grove, 106
Coldwater Recreation Area, 33
Collier Inn, 86
Conch House Restaurant, 1, 10
Conchs, 131
Conch Tour Train, 115, 131
Conservancy Nature Center,
    73, 89
Constitution Convention
    Museum, 25
Coral Gables, 108
Corkscrew Swamp Wildlife
    Sanctuary, 73, 90
Cornell Fine Arts Museum, 47

About the Authors

Diana and Bill Gleasner, an award-winning writer/photographer team, have thirty published books to their credit as well as hundreds of articles for national and international magazines and newspapers. As professional travel photo-journalists who have roamed the globe in search of fascinating travel experiences, they admit a continuing addiction to Florida. The Gleasners are members of the Society of American Travel Writers, Travel Journalists Guild, American Society of Magazine Photographers, and the American Society of Journalists and Authors.

Also of Interest from The Globe Pequot Press

Dixie: A Traveler's Guide $14.95
Discover the romance and charm of Dixie's antebellum past.

The Best Bike Rides in the South $12.95
A selective guide to the most beautiful and rigorous bike rides in the
south

Outlet Guide to the South, Third Edition $10.95
Factory outlets and their locations around the region

Recommended Country Inns: The South, Third Edition $14.95
The best inns in the region

Family Adventure Guide: Florida $11.95
Great things for the entire family to see and do in the Sunshine State

Southern Lighthouses $19.95
More than 50 lighthouses located along the entire southern coastline of
the U.S.

Other titles in this series:
Off the Beaten Path™ guides are available for every state in the
country and parts of Canada.

Available from your bookstore or directly from the publisher. For a free
catalogue or to place an order, call toll-free 24 hours a day (1-800-243-
0495), or write to The Globe Pequot Press, P.O. Box 833, Old Saybrook, Connecticut 06475-0833.